S0-AZY-740

SPORTS
Matters of Fact

Lamaine Honda

SPORTS
Matters of Fact

By Damaine Vonada

R 796.0977 V898
    NOR   0001813283858
Vonada, Damaine.

Sports matters of fact :
[Orange Frazer's Ohio
c1994. $14.95

Orange Frazer Press
Wilmington, Ohio

LORAIN PUBLIC LIBRARY
LORAIN, OHIO 44052

Copyright © 1994
by Orange Frazer Press
All rights reserved

No part of this publication may be reproduced
in any form without permission
from the publisher, unless
by a reviewer who wishes to quote briefly.

Library of Congress Catalog
Card Number: 94-066497

ISBN 1-882203-00-3

Published by Orange Frazer Press
37¹/₂ W. Main Street, Box 214
Wilmington, Ohio 45177

Staff
Brian Zampier, *illustration*
Brooke Wenstrup, *design*
Maria Britt, *editorial assistant*
Monica Vonada, *editorial assistant/Notre Dame
        research*

Contributors
James Baumann, for *Fast Company*
        and *Top Bucks*
Cassie Ring, for *Watermarks*
John Baskin and John Fleischman
        for *The Brash Menagerie*
Jodi Miller, cover photograph

Acknowledgments
John Heisler, Sports Information Director,
        University of Notre Dame

CONTENTS

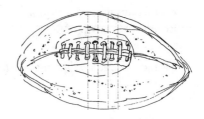

"*The moments of splendor, the ruthlessness of injury, the private inner sanctum of one's naked feeling exposed in loss or victory, the humor and tragedy of men at play and work can never be captured totally in words or pictures.*"

—*Ara Parseghian, coach at Miami of Oxford*

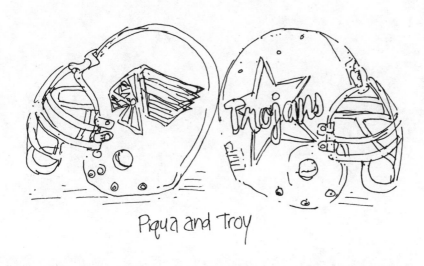

Piqua and Troy

SPORTS
Matters of Fact

♦ *The Akron Pros were professional football's first official champions, an honor earned in 1920 for having the best team record in the old American Professional Football Association. There wasn't a championship playoff game per se until 1932, when the Chicago Bears beat the Portsmouth Spartans in Chicago Stadium.*

First black American to win a gold medal in the Olympics—Cincinnati native William DeHart Hubbard, in the long jump (24' 5 1/8"), 1924

♦ *First pro football champion team*—Akron Pros, 1920

First pro football player trade—1920, when Akron sold tackle Bob "Nasty" Nash to the Buffalo All-Americans for $500 plus a percentage of the gate

First pro football playoff game—Chicago Bears 9, Portsmouth (Ohio) Spartans 0, December 18, 1932

First major pro football team with an unbeaten, untied season—1948 Cleveland Browns, who went 15–0, including the All-America Football Conference championship

First National Football League player to rush for 10,000 career yards—Jim Brown, Cleveland Browns, 1964

First Ohio player to win an NFL season rushing title—Cleveland Browns' Marion Motley, 810 yards, in 1950

First Ohio player to win an NFL season passing title—Cleveland Rams' Parker Hall, 1,227 yards, in 1939

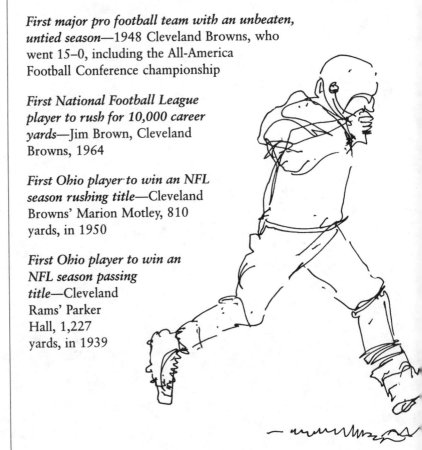

First Ohio player to win an NFL season title for receptions—
Cleveland Browns' Mac Speedie, 62 receptions, in 1952

First Ohio player to win an NFL season scoring title—
Cleveland Browns' Lou Groza, 77 points, in 1957

First players coached by football's legendary John Heisman—
Oberlin College Yeomen, who had a 7–0 season, 1892

*First Big Ten school to field football teams in all major college
Bowl games (Rose, Orange, Cotton, Sugar, and Fiesta)—*
Ohio State, 1921–1987

First Big Ten quarterback to win the Heisman Trophy—
Les Horvath, Ohio State, 1944

*"Never worry
about missing
a field goal.
Just blame the
holder and think
about kicking
the next one."*

—Lou Groza

*First football player (and one of only two in the NFL)
to catch ten or more passes in a Super Bowl*—Bengals' Dan
Ross, 11 receptions for 104 yards and two touchdowns, during
Cincinnati's 1982 loss to San Francisco

♦ *First black professional football player*—Wooster's Charles
W. Follis, signed as a halfback with the Shelby (Ohio) Athletic
Club, 1904

*First collegiate football player to rush for more than 4,000
yards and pass for more than 2,000*—Chris Spriggs,
at Denison University in Granville, 1986

*First sports souvenir shop in the U.S. devoted to a high school
team*—the Tiger Store in Massillon, founded 1973.

First woman to purchase a major league team—Cincinnati's
Marge Schott, Cincinnati Reds, 1984

*First President to play hooky from the White House and go
out to a ball game*—North Bend native Benjamin Harrison,
who watched his home state's Cincinnati Reds best
Washington, 7–4, in 1892

First major league baseball team to attract two million fans—
1948 Cleveland Indians

*First former major league player to become a major league
announcer*—Jack Graney, who followed the Indians'
play-by-play from 1932–1954

*First American League player to hit a home run his first time
at bat in a major league game*—Cleveland Indians' Earl Averill,
off Detroit's Earl Whitehill, April 16, 1929

First released pro baseball player—Richard Hurley, the $600
per season substitute ousted by the Cincinnati Reds, 1870

♦ THE CYCLONE

When he played football for the Wooster Athletic Association in the 1901, *CHARLES FOLLIS* was so fast that folks called him the "Black Cyclone." He was the son of a Virginia farmer who settled in Wooster. Charles helped start the football team at Wooster High School, and was elected captain. Frank Schiffer, manager of the Shelby Athletic Association, and signed Follis to a professional contract in 1904, and in his first game, he ran 83 yards for a touchdown, as Shelby beat Marion 29–0. One of Follis's teammates was Branch Rickey, who is said to have admired the dignified way Follis handled the many racial slurs directed at him. Years later, when Rickey decided to integrate modern major league baseball, he supposedly looked for a man with those same qualities and found them in Jackie Robinson.

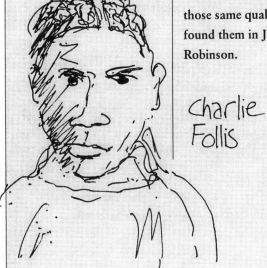

Charlie Follis

> "The only thing anybody seems to remember is that I once made an unassisted triple play in the World Series . . . You'd think I was born the day before, and died the day after."
>
> —Bill Wambsganss

First southpaw pitcher in pro baseball—Cincinnati-born Bobby Mitchell, who played for the Reds in the 1877 and 1878 seasons

First major league relief pitcher to play in 90 games in one season—Wayne Granger, Cincinnati Reds, 1969

First pinch hit in an All-Star game—Earl Averill's single off Lon Warneke, July 6, 1933

First opening day no-hitter (game of nine innings or more that a pitcher completes without allowing a hit)—pitched by the Cleveland Indians' Bob Feller, 1–0 over the White Sox, in Chicago's Comiskey Park, April 16, 1940

First unassisted triple play in the major leagues—Cleveland's Neal Ball, July 19, 1909

First unassisted triple play in a World Series game—Bill Wambsganss, Cleveland Indians, October 10, 1920

First grand slam home run in a World Series game—hit by Cleveland Indians' right fielder Elmer Smith, October 10, 1920

First Ohio player to win the major league's season batting average title—Cleveland's Nap Lajoie, .355 (tied with Pittsburgh's Honus Wagner), in 1903

First Ohio player to win the major league's season home run title—Cincinnati's Sam Crawford, 16 homers (tied with Philadelphia's Socks Seybold), in 1902

First Ohio player to win the major league's season RBI title—Cleveland's Nap Lajoie, 102 runs batted in, 1904

"Go up there and hit what you see. If you can't see it, come on back."

—Bucky Harris, Washington Senators manager, to his players facing Bob Feller

Bob Feller

• After Johnny Vander Meer's astounding feat of pitching, his endorsements climbed to slightly over $10,000.

First Ohio player to win the major league's season stolen bases title—Cincinnati's Bobby Tolan, 70 steals, 1970

First Ohio player to win the major league's season pitching title—Cleveland's Jim Bagby, won .721 of his games, 1920

First pitcher to hit a World Series home run—the Cleveland Indians' Jim Bagby, October 10, 1920

♦ First major league pitcher with back-to-back no-hitters—Cincinnati Reds' Johnny Vander Meer, against the Braves and Dodgers, June 11 and 15, 1938

First Ohio major leaguers to steal 30 bases and hit 30 home runs in one season—Cincinnati Reds' Eric Davis and Cleveland Indians' Joe Carter, both in 1987

First ex-major leaguer (and Cleveland Indian) to play in Japan—Larry Doby, who signed with the Chunichi Dragons, June 23, 1962

First American League player to pinch-hit a grand-slam home run—Cleveland Indians' Martin Cavanaugh, on Sept. 24, 1916

First National League team to stay in first place from the beginning to end of a 162-game season—Cincinnati Reds, 1990

First black college baseball player—Simpson Younger, Oberlin College, 1867

♦♦ First black major league baseball player—Mt. Pleasant's Moses Fleetwood Walker, Toledo Blue Stockings, 1884

First black coach of a modern pro basketball team— future Denver Rockets coach and Basketball Hall of Famer John McLendon, Cleveland Pipers, 1961

First black basketball coach at a major integrated university—John McLendon, Cleveland State University, 1966

♦♦ BLACK BALL

Born in 1857, *MOSES FLEETWOOD WALKER* played baseball at Oberlin College before making history as the first black in the major leagues when he joined the American Association's Toledo team in 1884. A bare-handed catcher, Walker lasted only one season with the Blue Stockings because of an injury, but he paved the way in baseball for other black players, including his brother and Blue Stockings team-mate Welday Wilberforce Walker. Racial bigotry was openly encouraged by white players such as Chicago White Stockings superstar (and future Hall-of-Famer) Cap Anson, integration of major league baseball was short-lived, and blacks were banned from playing for better—or in this case, worse—than half a century.

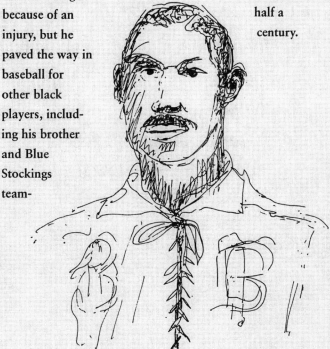

> *"Get that nigger off the field."*
>
> —*Cap Anson*

♦ *Oscar Robertson played above the ability of others yet tried to start each game by doling out an assist to his team-mates. This approach made him the NBA leader in assists until Magic Johnson finally broke the record in 1991. Oscar had 9,887 assists. He figured if his statisticians had used today's more liberal guidelines, he'd have had another six or seven thousand.*

Oscar Robertson

First National Basketball Association forward to average 30 points per game in one season—Cincinnati Royals' Jack Twyman, averaged 31.2 points per game, 1959–60

First player to get six steals in an NBA championship game—John Havlicek, of Bridgeport and the Boston Celtics, on May 3, 1974, against the Milwaukee Bucks

First men's collegiate basketball team—organized at Mount Union College in Alliance by trustee Herbert Jones, 1892

First state since 1910 with boasting rights to three consecutive men's collegiate basketball champions—Ohio, courtesy Ohio State in 1960 and the University of Cincinnati in 1961 and 1962

♦ *First sophomore to own the NCAA scoring title*—Oscar Robertson, University of Cincinnati, who averaged 35.1 points per game in 1957–58

First basketball player named an All-American for three years in high school and three more in college—Jerry Lucas, at Middletown and Ohio State

First American Indian to play professional baseball—James Madison Toy, Cleveland, American Association, 1887

First black major league manager—Frank Robinson, Cleveland Indians, 1975

First major league player to hit a home run off Babe Ruth—Cleveland Indians' Jack Graney, on June 11, 1914, when Ruth pitched for the Boston Red Sox

First jockey to win the Kentucky Derby five times—Eddie Arcaro of Cincinnati, in 1938, 1941, 1945, 1948, and 1952.

First Ohio high schooler drafted by a National Hockey League team—Mark Smith from Cleveland's Trinity High School, picked by Winnipeg Jets, 1988

For NBA players 6' 8" or under, Jerry Lucas still holds four of the top five spots in highest rebound average—he was 21.1, 20.0, 19.1, and 19.0 between 1964 and 1967 with Cincinnati. The Lakers' Elgin Baylor was third with 19.8 in 1960, and Detroit's Dennis Rodman with 18.7 in 1991 was sixth.

SECOND BANANAS

These players also ran, jumped, hit, swung, and, of course, scored

◆ The Browns' first choice in the 1957 draft was future Hall of Fame quarterback Len Dawson. But when the Browns lost a coin toss to Pittsburgh, they fortuitously obtained future Hall of Famer Jim Brown instead.

National Football League player with second-highest number of touchdowns scored rushing—Cleveland Browns' Jim Brown, 106

◆ Second choice of the Cleveland Browns in the 1957 draft—Jim Brown

Second Super Bowl player to score a touchdown on a kickoff return—Stanford Jennings, Cincinnati Bengals, 1989

◆ ◆ Second black major league player—Larry Doby, Cleveland Indians, 1947

Second hitter to get a National League home run—the Cincinnati Reds' Charley Jones, against Chicago, May 2, 1876

Second pitcher to save at least 20 games in both of his first major league seasons—Rawley Eastwick, Cincinnati Reds, 1975, 1976

Second winningest National Basketball Association coach—Lenny Wilkens, who racked up his 869th regular season victory at the helm of the Cleveland Cavaliers, 1993

Second youngest Masters golf tournament winner—Jack Nicklaus, at age 23 years, 2 months, and 16 days, in 1963

Second golfer to win the Professional Golf Association championship five times—Jack Nicklaus, 1963–1980

Second lowest British Open 72-hole total score—269, by Jack Nicklaus in 1977, the same year that Tom Watson got the record-low 268

Second jockey to win the Belmont Stakes six times—Cincinnati's Eddie Arcaro, in 1941, 1942, 1945, 1948, 1952, and 1955

Second quarterback in NFL history to throw TD passes in both·an AFC and an NFC Championship game—Boardman's Bernie Kosar, with Cleveland and Dallas

♦ ♦ COLORS

Only a few months after Jackie Robinson broke major league baseball's color barrier by joining the Brooklyn Dodgers in 1947, Cleveland Indians owner Bill Veeck tapped *LARRY DOBY* from the Negro National League. The 23-year-old out-fielder was not only the second black player in the major leagues, but first in the American League. His top notch performance with the Indians landed him in seven All-Star games, and he led the American League twice in home runs and once in RBIs. His .301 batting average in 1948 was also a major assist for the World Series-winning Indians. In 1978, when he took charge of the Chicago White Sox for part of the season, Doby become the second black major league manager. Ironically he was again following in the footsteps of a Robinson—Frank Robinson, who broke the managerial color barrier with the Cleveland Indians in 1975.

Bill Veeck
and
Larry Doby

" If U.S. Grant had been leading an army of baseball players, they'd have second-guessed him all the way to the doorknob of the Appomattox Courthouse."

—Bill Veeck

"It's not the customary thing to run around and smack into other people. Not everybody wants to do it."

—*Chuck Noll*

Most consecutive unbeaten regular season games by a National Football League team—the Canton Bulldogs' 25 (22 won, three tied) during the 1921–1923 seasons

Highest NFL career average in passing yards gained—8.63 by Otto Graham of the Cleveland Browns, 1950–1955

Highest NFL career average in rushing yards gained—5.22, by Jim Brown of the Cleveland Browns, 1957–1965

Youngest person inducted into the Pro Football Hall of Fame—Jim Brown, at age 35, 1971

Most NFL games played by a linebacker—232, Clay Matthews, Cleveland Browns (traded to Atlanta, 1994)

Most winning Super Bowl coach—Cleveland native and Browns veteran Chuck Noll, who took the Pittsburgh Steelers to four Super Bowl victories, in 1975, 1976, 1979, and 1980

Most pass receptions in a Super Bowl—11, by the Cincinnati Bengals' Dan Ross, 1982

Longest Super Bowl punt—63 yards, by the Cincinnati Bengals' Lee Johnson, 1989

Most consecutive National Collegiate Athletic Association Division I-A games with touchdown receptions—12, Cleveland's Desmond Howard, at the University of Michigan, 1990–1991

Most consecutive NCAA Division I-A games with pass receptions—44, by Gary Williams of Ohio State, 1979–82

"*I got clobbered in one game and had to have a bunch of stitches taken on my lip inside my mouth. Paul had the equipment guy weld a bar across my helmet. It was so thick I could hardly see around it to pass. But I think that's how the face mask started.*"

—*Otto Graham*

Otto
Graham

29

TALL TALE

♦ *Most points scored by a player in a National Collegiate Athletic Association game—113, by Clarence "Bevo" Francis of Rio Grande College, against Hillsdale College, February 2, 1954*

♦ Lanky, homespun **BEVO FRANCIS** was an unlikely basketball hero. True, he stood six feet 8 inches and had averaged 31 points per game at Wellsville High, but he was also the son of a struggling farmer—who bestowed him his nickname because of the popular soft drink "Beeve"—in Ohio's hardscrapple hill country. When Francis followed his high school coach Newt Oliver to Rio Grande College near Gallipolis, he didn't even have his high school diploma. He did, however, have a young wife and a new baby. When Francis got to Rio Grande the school was on the verge of bankruptcy. The gym roof leaked so badly that water puddled on the basketball court, and Mrs. Francis washed the team uniforms. In his first semester, Francis averaged almost 47 points a game and became a nationally known shooting star early in 1953, when he scored an incredible 116 points against Ashland Junior College of Kentucky. The NCAA, however, refused to recognize the record because Ashland was not a four year school. Oliver, meanwhile, was busy not only coaching Francis but also promoting him. The next year, with some help from teammates who fed him the ball, Francis staged another seemingly impossible performance by scoring 38 field goals and 37 free throws to rack up 113 points against Hillsdale. It was an indisputable NCAA record, and the publicity machine that Oliver set in motion went full-steam ahead. The national press declared Francis "the most outstanding basketball player in the world today," and he even made an appearance on Ed Sullivan's television show. Suddenly, Francis, Oliver, and Rio Grande were on the map and in the money. The college could finally afford to buy the team meals when they played away games. Oliver and Francis both left Rio Grande for the Boston Whirlwinds, the exhibition team that toured with the Harlem Globetrotters. But as much as he loved basketball, Francis hated the spotlight and traveling. He played professionally only a few years before going back home to his family.

Bevo Francis

> *"I have four or five systems but I usually use one where Bevo gets every shot."*
>
> —Newt Oliver, Rio Grande coach

"I wasn't afraid
of anybody
I'd seen in the
batter's box.
I'd been around
too long for that.
I wasn't as fast
as I used to be,
but I was a
better pitcher.
If I couldn't
overpower them,
I'd outcute
them."

—Satchel Paige, on his
major league premiere

Major league baseball player with most hits in World Series games—Cincinnati native Pete Rose, 45, garnered with the Reds in 1970, 1972, 1973, 1975, 1976, and with the Phillies in 1980, 1983

Major league baseball player with most hits and singles in a single game—John Burnett of the Cleveland Indians, who had 9 and 7 respectively in an 18-inning game, July 10, 1932

Major leaguer with highest World Series batting average in at least four games—the Cincinnati Reds' Billy Hatcher, .750, in the 1990 series against Oakland

Major league pitcher with the most career losses—Tuscarawas County native Cy Young, 313

Major league pitcher with the most career hits—Cy Young, with 623 hits in 2,960 at-bats for a .210 average

Major leaguer with most innings pitched and most games completed in a season—the Cincinnati Reds' Will White, with 680 and 75 respectively, in 1879

Oldest rookie in the major leagues—Satchel Paige, who was 42 when he joined the Cleveland Indians in 1948

Youngest major league baseball player in the twentieth century—Cincinnati Reds pitcher Joe Nuxhall, who took the mound at age 15, in 1944

Youngest manager to head a major league team from the beginning of the baseball season—24-year-old Lou Boudreau, who became chief of the Cleveland Indians in 1942

Oldest modern major league player to hit a grand-slam home run—the Cincinnati Reds' Tony Perez, at age 43, 1985

Largest crowd to attend a major league doubleheader— 84,587, who watched the Indians mop up the Yankees 4–1 and 3–2, on September 12, 1954

Largest winning margin by a National Basketball Association team— the Cleveland Cavaliers' searing, 68-point spearing of the Miami Heat, December 17, 1991

Most holes of golf played (via a cart) in 24 hours— 846, by David Cavalier, at North Canton's Arrowhead Country Club, August 6–7, 1990

Most years as golf's top money winner— 8, for Columbus native Jack Nicklaus, in 1964, 1965, 1967, 1971, 1972, 1973, 1975, 1976

Most Grand Slam golf championships— 18, by Jack Nicklaus, who has won six Masters, four U.S. Opens, three British Opens, and five Professional Golfers Association tournaments

Lowest 72-hole score in the U.S. Open— 272, by Jack Nicklaus at Baltusrol Country Club in New Jersey, 1980

Most Preakness Stakes wins— 6, by Cincinnati's Eddie Arcaro, in the 1941, 1948, 1950, 1951, 1955, and 1957 races

Highest Women's International Bowling Congress individual three-game score— 864, by Cleveland's Jeanne Maiden, in Solon, November 23, 1986

Most WIBC consecutive strikes— 40, by Jeanne Maiden, in Solon, November 23, 1986

Most perfect bowling games (300 points), women— 19, by Jeanne Maiden in Ladies Professional Bowlers Tour events

♦ *Most perfect bowling games (300 points), men—* 45, by Mike Whalin of Cincinnati, 1994

♦ **MIKE WHALIN'S NUMBERS**

His average: 223

Most 300 games in a season: 12 (a record)

Best three-game series: 857

Number of bowling balls in his car: 20

Number of games he bowls each week: 75-100

♦ *Ohio and Illinois players thought their 1943 football contest was over and were already in their dressing rooms, when officials ruled Illinois was offside on the last play. Because of the penalty, the teams went back on the field after the clock had run out, and Buckeye freshman John Stungis—who had never before attempted one— kicked a field goal that gave the Buckeyes a 29–26 victory.*

Only National Football League coach to take two different teams to the Super Bowl—Grand River native Don Shula, in 1969 with Baltimore, and in 1972, 1973, 1974, 1983, and 1985 with Miami

Only Ohio college player who became a starting quarterback in a Super Bowl game—Youngstown State's Ron Jaworski, for the Philadelphia Eagles in the 1980 Super Bowl

Only starting football player in four consecutive Rose Bowl games—running back Archie Griffin of Ohio State, 1973, 1974, 1975, 1976

Only Big Ten team to win an Orange Bowl—Ohio State, which defeated Colorado 27–10, in 1977

♦ *Only "fifth quarter" football game played at Ohio State*— November 13, 1943; OSU over Illinois, 29–26

Only father-and-son college football coaches to win National Collegiate Athletic Association championships—dad, Lee Tressel, who guided Baldwin-Wallace College to its 1978 Division III title, and son, Jim Tressel, coach of Youngstown State's 1991 Division I-AA team

Only Ohio college with three consecutive unbeaten, untied NCAA Division I-A football seasons—University of Toledo, which went 11–0 in 1969, 12–0 in 1970, and 12–0 in 1971

Only major leaguer to hit home runs from both sides of home plate in the same inning—the Cleveland Indians' Carlos Baerga, in the seventh inning on April 9, 1993, when he batted right-handed to hit a two-run homer off Yankee relief pitcher Steve Howe and then batted left-handed for another homer off Steve Farr

Only major league pitcher to win 200 games in both leagues— Cy Young, with 289 National League and 222 American League victories

Only major league outfielder to play in each of the first six All-Star games—the Cleveland Indians' Earl Averill

Only catcher to hold batting titles from both major leagues—Ernie Lombardi, who batted .342 with the Cincinnati Reds in 1938 and .330 with the Boston Braves in 1942

Only team to get four consecutive perfect at-bats—Cleveland Indians, on July 31, 1963, when California Angels pitcher Paul Foytack allowed Woodie Held, Pedro Ramos, Tito Francona, and Larry Brown four home runs in a row

Don Shula

"Shula can take his'n and beat your'n or he can take your'n and beat his'n."

—*Bum Phillips on Don Shula*

Only Ohio player—and one of only a handful of major leaguers—to hit 20 or more doubles, triples, and home runs in one season—the Cleveland Indians' Jeff Heath, who had 32 doubles, 20 triples, and 24 home runs in 1941

Only double no-hitter in the major leagues—the nine-inning pitching duel between Cincinnati's Fred Toney and Chicago's Jim Vaughn on May 2, 1917, which the Reds won 1–0 after Vaughn surrendered two hits and one run in the tenth inning.

Only person to both play on and coach NCAA Division I championship basketball teams—former Orrville resident Bobby Knight, who played with the 1960 Ohio State champs and coached the Indiana Hoosiers to titles in 1976, 1981, and 1987

Only Ohio State basketball player who was a three-time All-American and three-time Big Ten Most Valuable Player—Jerry Lucas, 1960–1962

Only NCAA Division I basketball teams from the same state to play each other in the men's championship game—University of Cincinnati and Ohio State (Cincinnati won 70–65 in 1961, and 71–59 in 1962)

Only NCAA Division I tennis champion from an Ohio college—Tony Trabert, University of Cincinnati, 1951

♦ *Only jockey to win horse racing's Triple Crown (Kentucky Derby, Preakness Stakes, Belmont Stakes) twice*—Cincinnati native Eddie Arcaro, riding Whirlaway in 1941, and Citation in 1948

Only woman to ever umpire a game between two major league teams—Pam Postema, Willard

Only man to homer in his first two times at bat in the major leagues—Cincinnatian Bob Nieman, with the St. Louis Browns in 1951

SWEET RIDE

♦ **EDDIE ARCARO** learned to ride at the Latonia track not far from his Cincinnati birthplace. Considered too small for scholastic sports—he wanted to play baseball— he left school at the age of 13 and got a job as exercise boy at a racetrack. Soon, he discovered that his 5' 2" frame was just right for racing horses, and only two years after dropping out of school, the teen-age Arcaro was riding professionally. He went on to win horse racing's Triple Crown—the Kentucky Derby, the Preakness Stakes, and the Belmont Stakes—twice. He won all his Triple Crown races by nothing less than a full length, which meant he kept faith with his own credo: "Don't get beat by no noses." In 1948, he became the first jockey in history to amass $1 million worth of racing victories in a single year. Although Arcaro called *Whirlaway* his most exciting horse, it was on *Citation* that he made history— becoming the only jockey to win two Triple Crowns. By the time Arcaro retired in 1962, he had ridden more than 24,000 horses, won 4,779 races, and accumulated more than $30 million in purse money. A canny businessman, Arcaro invested his share of the purses so wisely and well that his agent once observed, "He's the only jockey who subscribes to the *Racing Form* and the *Wall Street Journal*."

"I lost my cap and finished with the tail of my silks coming out of my pants."

—Eddie Arcaro on his first race, age 15, at Bainbridge Park in Cleveland, May 18, 1931

> *"After what I went through the last couple of years, I stopped reading the papers. I was scared they were going to say I started the Gulf War."*
>
> —*Pete Rose*

Last year a pro football team won the National Foorball League championship and had a player who won the NFL rushing title—1964, when Jim Brown rushed 1,446 yards to help put the Cleveland Browns at the top of the NFL's heap

Last time the Cleveland Browns won their first three games of the season—1979, when they beat the New York Jets, Kansas City, and Baltimore

Last player to score five touchdowns during a National Collegiate Athletic Association Division I-A game—Dan Rebsch of Miami University, November 4, 1972

Last player to get field goals in 19 consecutive NCAA Division I-A games—Gary Gussman of Miami University, 1986–1987

♦ *Last day of Joe DiMaggio's all-time, record-setting, 56-game hitting streak*—July 16, 1941, in Cleveland

Last Cleveland Indian to start in two consecutive All-Star games—Al Rosen, 1953 and 1954

Last major league player-manager—Pete Rose of the Cincinnati Reds, 1984–1987

Pete Rose

THE STREAK

♦ In the last innocent American summer before Pearl Harbor, the legendary New York Yankee JOE DIMAGGIO had a record-setting hitting streak that captured the entire nation's attention. Beginning May 15, 1941, he got 91 hits in 56 consecutive games, including 16 doubles, four triples, and 15 home runs. The Yankee Clipper's luck ran out at CLEVELAND STADIUM on July 17, when he couldn't get to first base against Indians pitchers Al Smith and Jim Bagby. In the eighth inning, Indian Lou Boudreau picked up a ground ball off DiMaggio's bat for a double play that ended his streak. The Yankees won 4–3, but there was no joy in New York, and little anywhere else. Many in the Cleveland crowd of 67,468 booed the Indians for what they did to DiMaggio. The *Plain Dealer*'s front page banner headline read: "DiMaggio Stopped, but Yankees Win." Ironically, it had been the Indians' Mel Harder who on May 14 was the last pitcher to send DiMaggio home hitless before his history-making hitting streak began. "The memory of that game is very clear to me, very clear," said DiMaggio. " Strangely enough, I wanted to keep on going. I felt a little downhearted. I was stopped, but I quickly got over that. It was like going into the seventh game of the World Series and losing it. That's how I felt. But I did want to keep on going. I wanted it to go on forever."

Last time Ohio State's football team had the Number 1 ranking in the Associated Press pre-season poll—1980

Last Ohio State football player named a Rhodes Scholar—Mike Lanese, 1985

Last major league player-manager to win a pennant—Lou Boudreau, who took the Cleveland Indians to the American League and World Series Championships in 1948

Last brother-brother battery (pitcher and catcher) in a major league game—pitcher Jim Bailey and catcher Ed Bailey, who were siblings sans rivalry for the Cincinnati Reds, September 10, 1959

Last major leaguer to pitch two complete games in one day—the Cleveland Indians' Dutch Levsen, who beat Boston 6–1 and 5–1, August 28, 1926

Last Cleveland Indian to lead the American League in earned run average—Rick Sutcliffe, 2.96 ERA, 1982

Last American League player to hit three consecutive triples in a single game—the Cleveland Indians' Ben Chapman, on July 2, 1939

Last out for the Indians in their last game at Cleveland Stadium—made by shortstop Mark Lewis of Hamilton, who struck out, as the White Sox shut out the Indians 4–0, October 3, 1993

The last game that the legendary Cy Young ever pitched—for the Boston Braves on October 6, 1911; he played $6^1/_3$ innings, gave up 11 hits, and lost 13–3 to the Brooklyn Dodgers

FAMOUS LAST WORDS

"This is my last slide."
—*one-time Cincinnati ballplayer, Mike "King" Kelly, on his deathbed*

"What did the Reds do?"
—*Warren G. Harding, on his deathbed*

"You can't interview me here."
—*what Ted Turner, Braves owner and native Cincinnatian, says he wishes on his tombstone*

"Tell Mays not to worry."
—*Ray Chapman, Cleveland Indians infielder, after getting hit in the head by pitcher Carl Mays in 1920*

" I resigned, but it came as a surprise to me."
—*newly ousted Cleveland Indians' president Rick Bay, 1992*

*"My eyes are very misty
As I pen these words
to Christy;
O, my heart is full
of heaviness today.
May the flowers
n'er wither, Matty,
On your grave
at Cincinnati,
Which you've
chosen for your final
fade-away."*
*—Ring Lardner,
sportswriter, on
NY Giants pitcher
Christy Mathewson
who retired to manage
the Reds, 1916*

" If I go, I want it to be in the Blitzen Benz, or a faster car if they ever build one, with my foot holding the throttle wide open. I want the grandstand to be crowded and the band playing the latest rag. I want them all to say, as they file out the gate, 'Well, old Barney—he was goin' some!' "
—*Barney Oldfield*

THE PROS

CLEVELAND INDIANS

In the 1870s, Cleveland's first baseball team with professional players was the short-lived Forest Citys, which borrowed its name from a previous pro-am baseball club that originally had taken the name from Cleveland's "Forest City" sobriquet. Next came the Spiders, whose tall, thin players supposedly crawled all over other teams in the 1880s and 1890s. In 1900, American League founder Ban Johnson moved a minor league team that wore bright blue uniforms from Iowa to Cleveland, and those Blues became the forerunners of today's Indians. When Napoleon Lajoie, a well-liked hitter with a big batting average, started managing the Blues in 1901, they were called the Naps. After Lajoie's departure in 1914, a newspaper contest to rename the team resulted in Indians at the suggestion of a fan who wanted to honor Louis Sockalexis, an Indian who had played outfield for the Spiders. "Chief" Sockalexis thus became the first—and only—person for whom a major league team is named.

CINCINNATI REDS

When the Cincinnati Baseball Club openly went professional in 1869, the team's socks made Red Stockings an obvious nickname, although some dubbed the players Porkopolitans because of Cincinnati's well-known hog industry. The club's name was shortened to Reds in 1881, when it forsook the National League, which did not condone selling beer at games, to join the new American Association, which did. In the 1950s, the Cold War and McCarthyism gave "Reds" a meaning that had nothing to do with baseball, and the team obligingly adopted the nickname Redlegs as a politically correct step in the nation's march against communism. But by 1960, the Reds were once again their old colorful selves, and have remained the Reds ever since.

CLEVELAND BROWNS AND CINCINNATI BENGALS

Both of Ohio's pro football teams have a Paul Brown connection. When Cleveland businessman Mickey McBride got a National Football League franchise in the 1944, he drummed up interest in the team by holding a contest to name it. The people's overwhelming choice was "Browns" after the phenomenally successful Massillon and Ohio State coach, Paul Brown. McBride then sealed the deal by giving Brown the sweetest contract ever offered any pro football coach up to that time: $20,000 per season plus fifteen percent of the profits. Brown, of course, paid McBride back handsomely by turning the Browns into one of the most successful NFL teams of the 1940s and 1950s. After Art Modell took over the team and fired him in the early 1960s, Brown started a new NFL franchise in Cincinnati. He called the team "Bengals," reviving a name used by Cincinnati's defunct American Football League franchises of 1937, 1940, and 1941.

TOLEDO MUD HENS

A farm team for the Detroit Tigers, the Mud Hens were made famous by Toledo native Jamie Farr, who played Corporal Klinger on M*A*S*H and remained a true blue fan come hell, high water, or the Korean War. Started more than a century ago, the ball club moved in and out of Toledo and nicknames several times before settling on the town and the sobriquet shortly after the turn of the century. The Mud Hens moniker is said to have originated when the team played at Bay View Park. Wild birds lived in the adjacent marshland, and one white-beaked species—the mud hen—dropped in from time to time during its migrations.

"I'm here to win. I'll make this team a winner if it takes every cent you've got. I'd rather win before 1,000 than lose in front of 8,000."

—Paul Brown
to Mickey McBride

HIGH SCHOOLS AND COLLEGES

"BATTLIN' BEAVERS"—Beavercreek High School, Greene County

"BIG RED"—Denison University

"BISHOPS"—Ohio Wesleyan University

"BLUE STREAKS"—John Carroll University

"BUCKEYES"—Ohio State University

"CERAMICS"—Crooksville High School, Perry County

"CRUSADERS"—Capital University

"FIGHTING MUSKIES"—Muskingum College

"FIGHTING QUAKERS"—Wilmington College

"FIGHTING SCOTS"—College of Wooster

"FIGHTING STUDENT PRINCES"—Heidelberg College

"FLYERS"—University of Dayton

"GOLDEN FLASHES"—Kent State University

"JEEPS"—South Webster High School, Scioto County

"LORDS" (and **"LADIES"**)—Kenyon College

"MARAUDERS"—Central State University

"MUSKETEERS"—Xavier University

"PENGUINS"—Youngstown State University

"PIONEERS"—Malone College

"POLAR BEARS"—Ohio Northern University

"PUNCHERS"—Mifflin High School, Columbus

"PURPLE RAIDERS"—Mount Union College

"REDSKINS"—Miami University

"ROCKETS"—University of Toledo

"SCARABS"—East Technical High School, Cleveland

"SHERMAN TANKS"—Union-Scioto High School (a.k.a. Unioto), Ross County

"TARBLOODERS"—Glenville High School, Cleveland

"TERRIERS"—Hiram College

"WHIPPETS"—Shelby High School, Richland County

"YELLOW JACKETS"—The Defiance College, Baldwin-Wallace College

"YEOMEN" (and **"YEOWOMEN"**)—Oberlin College

"ZEPS"—Shenandoah High School, Noble County

"ZIPS"—University of Akron

"If the name Redskins is not patently objectionable, how is it that no one seems to name their team the Palefaces?"

—*Tim Sullivan*

HUMBLE ORIGINS

♦ South Webster High School acquired its nickname in 1940, not from the World War II vehicle, but from "Eugene the Jeep," a Popeye comic strip character. After some local folks compared know-it-all Eugene with South Webster's basketball coach, the Portsmouth newspaper picked up on the "Jeep" joke, and by 1949, JEEPS was permanently emblazoned on the school's varsity uniforms.

♦ Shenandoah High School got its name and its teams were tagged the ZEPS because in 1925, the zeppelin Shenandoah crashed near the Noble County community where the school is located.

♦ In a poll taken by the Los Angeles Times in the 1970s, the FIGHTING STUDENT PRINCES was voted the nation's oddest collegiate nickname, beating out the Missouri Fighting Kangaroos for the honor. Heidelberg teams were called the Cardinals until 1926, when Edwin Butcher, a publicity man at the college, noticed an advertisement for the movie, The Student Prince of Heidelberg. Knowing a good gimmick when he saw one, Butcher began referring to the Student Princes in his press releases, and a novel nickname was born.

♦ ZIPS was suggested by University of Akron freshman Margaret Hamlin in 1926, because of the "Zippers" overshoes made by a local company, BFGoodrich.

♦ When Oberlin College began competing in intercollegiate athletics in 1886, only male students played the games. Varsity team members were awarded a letter "O" and referred to as "Ye, O Men," which soon became **YEOMEN**. After Oberlin's athletic program for female students began in 1973, the **YEOWOMEN** were a logical addition. In 1994, however, the Oberlin College baseball team included a woman, Erin Marks. This was considered entirely appropriate since Oberlin was the country's first coeducational college but it did have an effect on the team nickname: The Yeomen thus became **THE YEONINE**.

♦ The **MUSKETEERS** was chosen as Xavier University's nickname because of its noble connotations and the many connections that the school had to France during its early days. When the people of Auch, France learned about the nickname in the 1960s, they presented the university with a reproduction of the statue honoring their most famous native son, D'Artagnan, whom Alexandre' Dumas immortalized in The Three Musketeers.

OHIO'S TEN MOST POPULAR HIGH SCHOOL TEAM NICKNAMES:

1. Tigers
2. Panthers
3. Wildcats
4. Eagles/Golden Eagles
5. Bulldogs
6. Indians
7. Warriors/ Golden Warriors
8. Vikings
9. Falcons
10. Cardinals, Trojans (tie)

♦ **THE CANTON TEN—**
PRO FOOTBALL'S
CHARTER MEMBERS

Akron (Ohio) Pros

Canton (Ohio) Bulldogs

Cleveland (Ohio) Indians

Dayton (Ohio) Triangles

Decatur (Illinois) Staleys

Hammond (Indiana) Pros

Muncie (Indiana) Flyers

Racine (Illinois) Cardinals

Rochester (New York) Jeffersons

Rock Island (Illinois) Independents

♦ 1. PROFESSIONAL FOOTBALL

After the Civil War, amateur football teams sponsored by athletic clubs slowly acquired paid players, and by the turn of the century, there were a number of professional teams playing in Ohio and Pennsylvania. The first serious attempt to organize and bring respectability to those fledgling pro teams, which often employed college students playing under false names, occurred in Canton, Ohio, on September 17, 1920. In the showroom of his Hupmobile dealership, Canton Bulldogs business manager Ray Hay hosted a meeting during which the American Professional Football Association was officially organized and charter memberships were offered to ten teams. The league was reorganized and renamed the National Football League in 1922, and pro teams have been playing under its aegis ever since.

2. CENTER SNAP

Before 1893, when John Heisman became the coach at Buchtel College (now the University of Akron), football was a game in which the center *rolled* the ball across the ground to the quarterback. But the technique wasn't working well for the Akron team because 6' 4" quarterback Harry Clark couldn't reach the ball quickly enough. Heisman solved the problem by having the center *throw* the ball through his legs to the quarterback, a move that teams across the country soon copied and made a permanent part of the game.

3. SHOOT-AND-RUN OFFENSE

This much-used pro football strategy was devised by Glenn "Tiger" Ellison, who coached at Middletown High School from 1933–1963. To compensate for his small linemen and backs in the late 1950s, Ellison put his quarterback under the center and spread his other players across the field, thus effectively diluting the opponent's defense. Ellison wrote a book about the tactic, and it served as a primer for other coaches.

4. PENALTY FLAGS

In 1941, Youngstown College football coach Dike Beede gave flags made by his wife Irma to referees at the October 16 home game against Oklahoma City. He thought the flags would be a sane and silent alternative to the cacophony of horns and whistles that were then used to signal penalties and stop play. Referee Jack McPhee kept his flag, and a few years later, he used it in Columbus during the Ohio State–Iowa contest. The visiting Big Ten commissioner was so taken with the concept that the entire conference soon took up the cloth. Mrs. Beede's needlework made her the "Betsy Ross of Football," and McPhee's original flag ended up in college football's Hall of Fame.

5. LATEX MOUTHPIECE

The impression-molded mouthpiece routinely used by football players to protect their pearly whites was invented by a Columbus dentist, Dr. William Walton, Jr., in 1956. Dr. Walton first tested his device on his son's football teammates at Columbus Academy.

6. MONDAY NIGHT FOOTBALL

The weekly subject of television contention in many a household began with Cleveland Browns owner Art Modell. His teamwork with network TV resulted in pro football's first Monday meeting on September 21, 1970, in which the Browns beat the Jets 31–21 at Cleveland Stadium. The show that Modell made has since become one of prime time's biggest success stories, ranking seventh in viewer popularity during the 1992–1993 television season.

"Time was when we fooled the enemy by having the quarterback pass a tan helmet to one of his halfbacks and the ball to another."

—*John Heisman*

"Harry Wright is a base-ball Edison. He eats base-ball, breathes base-ball, thinks base-ball, dreams base-ball, and incorporates base-ball in his prayers."

—*Cincinnati Enquirer*

7. DETROIT LIONS

If it hadn't been for the Depression, Portsmouth, Ohio, might today be the home of a National Football League franchise. One of the first NFL franchises was the Portsmouth Spartans, which was owned by shoe manufacturer Homer Selby. Sparked by the all-around skills of all-pro tailback "Dutch" Clark, the Spartans had four rough and rollicking years in the NFL, playing in the first pro football championship game and cultivating a keen rivalry with the Green Bay Packers that drew thousands of fans. At the end of the 1933, season, however, the hard times were taking their toll at both the gate and the shoe company. Selby sold the Spartans to a Michigan businessman who moved the team to Detroit and in 1934 changed its name to Lions.

8. CATCHER'S CROUCH

Baseball catchers find themselves squatting behind the plate because of Cincinnatian Buck Ewing. New York's first super-star, Ewing is said to be the best player of the nineteenth century and credited with being, in the 1880s, the first to hunker down behind the plate. He was first to use a padded catcher's mitt, too.

9. PROFESSIONAL BASEBALL

In 1869, businessman George Ellard and the ambitious player Harry Wright organized the Cincinnati Red Stockings, the first baseball team to consist entirely of players who not only toured but also were paid for their sporting services. The payroll for the 10-man team totaled $9,300, and star shortstop George Wright (Harry's little brother) drew the club's top $1,400 salary. The team finished that seminal season with a 64–0–1 record.

10. AMERICAN LEAGUE

Today's mighty major league began in Cincinnati at the turn of the century, when Reds manager Charlie Comiskey and his friend Ban Johnson decided to strengthen a faltering minor league called the Western Association in order to challenge the powerful National League, which had a virtual monopoly on professional baseball. In 1894, Comiskey moved on to Chicago to do his own empire building, while Johnson, a former sports-writer for the *Cincinnati Commercial Gazette*, took over the Western League. Aggressive and even ruthless at times, Johnson single-mindedly forced the league's growth and expansion. He renamed it the American League and openly competed with the National League by pirating players and starting new ball clubs in cities that already had NL teams. The somewhat stuffy son of a Norwalk, Ohio, minister, Johnson also made great strides in making baseball a respectable spectator sport. Rowdiness in the stands was discouraged; beer sales were banned; players were forbidden to use profanity; and ball park fisticuffs were discouraged by installing professional umpires who had final authority in a game. Within a decade, Johnson had not only built the American League, but also had given it equal stature with the National League. The first World Series that Johnson instigated in 1903 was a byproduct of the National League's coming to terms with its competition. Fittingly, the Boston Red Sox of the upstart American League bested the National League's Pittsburgh Pirates, 5 games to 3. The single-minded Johnson remained the American League's president until 1927. He also was a member of the three-man National Commission—which, of course, he helped to create—that ran organized baseball until the 1919 Black Sox scandal eroded his authority and baseball's credibility.

11. THE BASEBALL MANAGER IN UNIFORM

Harry Wright of the 1869 Cincinnati Red Stockings was the first pro baseball manager to wear his team's uniform. Although his invention was a matter of necessity since he also played center field, baseball is still the only major sport in which the coach wears the same clothing as the players.

12. BASEBALL SOCKS AND KNEE-LENGTH PANTS

The major leagues' major garb was first worn by the Cincinnati Red Stockings. When the players started wearing their trademark long red socks in the late 1860s, they had to drop their long pants in favor of the shorter style still sported on today's diamonds.

13. BASEBALL UNIFORM NUMBERS

In 1883, Cincinnati Reds president Aaron Stern decided to designate his players by putting numbers on their uniforms instead of putting them in uniforms of different colors. Since only prison inmates wore numbers, many Reds thought the experiment was criminal. The Cleveland Indians then inaugurated the custom of putting numbers on the backs of baseball uniforms on April 6,

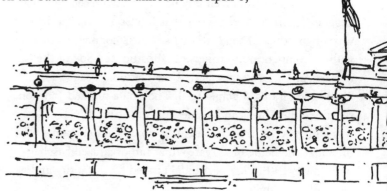

1929. Earl Averill stepped up to the plate sporting No. 5 on his back, and promptly hit a home run with his first at-bat.

◆ 14. SHIN GUARDS

In 1906, Cincinnati Reds trainer Mike Murphy devised a pair of rattan protectors for the much-injured shins of catcher Charles "Red" Dooin. A few years later, Toledo-born catcher Roger Bresnahan of the New York Giants had a run-in with Doonin and his shin guards at home plate, whereupon he ordered a pair for himself and popularized their use.

15. MODERN BALLPARK

The first major league baseball park designed with the spectators in mind was the Cincinnati Reds' elegant League Park, which was rebuilt in 1902 after a fire destroyed the original League Park. With theater boxes, double deck seating, and Corinthian columns, the ornate Beaux Arts building was such a far cry from the usual naked bleachers that it was dubbed "The Palace of the Fans." Happily, the new ballpark was also a far cry from the first League Park, which had been badly designed. The grandstand fell down after the first game, and the poorly positioned home plate

◆ Cincinnatian Red Dooin borrowed the idea for shin guards from English cricket players, but he was embarrassed to be seen with them in public—they weren't considered "manly"—and hid them under his uniform.

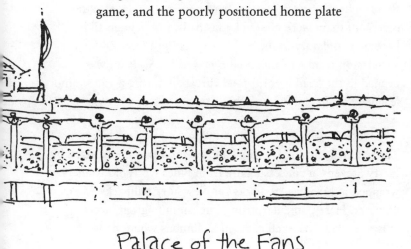

Palace of the Fans

subjected swatters to so much glare that an 1892 contest between the Reds and Boston was called on account of "excess sunshine."

16. BASEBALL BEAT REPORTER

The first writer assigned to cover a team on a full-time basis was Harry Millar, hired by the *Cincinnati Commercial* to follow the Red Stockings and report on their history-making 1869 travels.

17. BASEBALL PLAYERS AND CHEWING TOBACCO

The most obvious (and some say odious) personal practice in the major leagues is said to have originated with George Hemming, a moustachioed pitcher from Carrollton who played with the pennant-winning Baltimore Orioles in the late 1890s. Not only did he habitually eat grass while he pitched, he also grazed whenever his team scored a run. He ate so much grass, in fact, that his teammates claimed he had to be part Holstein.

18. BASEBALL HELMETS

In 1941, Brooklyn Dodgers owner and Ohio native Branch Rickey put the first protective hard hats on his players after several of them were injured by fastballs. But helmets didn't become mandatory in the major leagues until Don Zimmer, a shortstop from Cincinnati who played for St. Paul, was beaned in the head by near-fatal curveball during a 1953 minor league game in Columbus, Ohio.

19. HOT DOG

The nation's all-time favorite ballpark food was popularized by Harry Stevens, a concessionaire from Niles who sold wieners wrapped in bread as "red hots" at New York ballparks. First, however, Harry, an enterprising English immigrant, accidentally attended a baseball game in Columbus where he was so confused he cobbled together the first practical scorecard. The business expanded to other ballparks and his son, Frank, invented the bilingual scorecard, for German fans in Milwaukee, and Harry himself landed in New York. He got the contract for concessions at the polo grounds, where the Giants played, and where Scorecard Harry is said to have popularized soda pop by putting straws in the bottles, thus allowing the fervent fan to drink without missing any action on the field. But Harry really outdid himself when, on a cold day in 1901 at the polo grounds, he saw that the fans needed not soda but a hot sandwich; the hired help went off into the neighborhood and at Harry's bidding, bought up all the dachshund sausages and Vienna rolls they could find. A New York newspaper cartoonist, who couldn't spell "dachshund," caricatured the sandwich as a "hot dog," and American history was made. When Scorecard Harry died in 1934, he was brought home to Niles and buried in the Niles City Cemetery.

"You can't tell the players without a scorecard!"

—*Harry Stevens*

Harry Stevens

When baseball's noisy innovator and hothead, Larry MacPhail, struck Cincinnati in 1933, there were, one writer noted, more people in the hotel lobby than the ball park. MacPhail painted the park and performed stunts—he sat a refrigerator in centerfield and gave it to the first player who hit it. He also laid the groundwork for the pennants of 1939 and 1940. "My coffee tastes lousy the morning after we blow one," he liked to say.

20. NIGHT BASEBALL

The first major league game played under the lights was at Cincinnati's Crosley Field on May 24, 1935, a truly illuminating moment for the Reds (they beat the Phillies 2–1) and for baseball, courtesy of the promotion-minded club manager Larry MacPhail and President Franklin Roosevelt, who agreed to throw the switch. Several weeks later, on July 10, the Reds made history again when Babe Herman hit the first home run in a major league night game.

21. PRESIDENT THROWING OUT THE FIRST BASEBALL

The custom of inaugurating the baseball season by having the

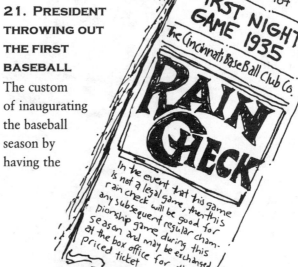

264
BOX
LOWER BOX
Est. Price $1.5.99
Fed. Tax .16
State Tax .0464
1.75
FIRST NIGHT GAME 1935
The Cincinnati BaseBall Club Co.

RAIN CHECK

In the event that this game is not a legal game, then this rain check will be good for any subsequent regular championship game during this season and may be exchanged at the box office for this priced ticket.

President of the United States toss the first ball began with William Howard Taft, a one-time sandlot catcher in Cincinnati, who officially did the honors for the Washington Senators on April 14, 1910.

22. GRAPEFRUIT LEAGUE

After Ohioan Branch Rickey discovered Florida's fine weather and ready supply of retirees to patronize his St. Louis practice games in 1914, the Sunshine State became the site where most major league teams conduct their spring training.

23. ARTIFICIAL FISH LURES

Akron's Ernest Pflueger pioneered the concept of luring fish with non-natural bait. He invented the first artificial fish lures in the 1880s and 1890s.

24. UMPIRES' HAND SIGNALS

An outstanding Cincinnati Reds outfielder at the turn of the century, William Ellsworth "Dummy" Hoy was also a deaf mute who could not understand the umpires when they called a ball or strike. At his suggestion, umpires raised the right hand to signal a strike and the left to signal a ball. Hoy thus handed baseball a significant legacy, which is far more than can be said for his contemporary and fellow deaf mute, Dummy Taylor. Taylor, who pitched for the New York Giants team that won the 1905 World Series, was once kicked out of the Polo Grounds for slandering an umpire . . . in sign language.

25. PUTTING ON ERRORS

The practice of placing errors on the scoreboard in plain view of the fans was another Larry MacPhail innovation. Mistakes by major leagues made their first appearance on the bottom corner of the Reds' Crosley Field scoreboard in 1934.

26. NCAA Championship Tournament

The annual playoff that is college basketball's equivalent of the Super Bowl and World Series began in 1939, the brainchild of Ohio State coach Harold Olsen, who first suggested it and served on the tournament's first committees. Ohio State, of course, participated in that first tournament, along with Oklahoma, Brown, Oregon, Texas, Utah State, Villanova, and Wake Forest. In the final game, Oregon bested Ohio State 46–33.

27. Crowley Rule

The first instant replay in college basketball occurred at the University of Dayton Arena during 1984's first round of play between Morehead State and North Carolina A&T. Official Mickey Crowley asked ESPN announcers to help determine which Aggie player should shoot from the foul line by rerunning the play. The Aggies won 69–68, and the NCAA subsequently enacted the Crowley rule that banned instant replay.

28. The popularization of golf

John D. Rockefeller maintained a nine-hole golf course on his Cleveland estate where in the late 1800s, he doggedly pursued a white ball with a club. Photos of him on the green appeared in newspapers for years, convincing Americans to follow him onto the links. Then in 1899, another Clevelander, Coburn Haskell, put a rubber core inside the golf ball to give it greater distance. When Akron's BFGoodrich company began manufacturing Haskell's invention, the commonly used gutta percha ball became obsolete. Haskell's revolutionary rubber ball went far, reducing golfers' scores and making the game even more popular and anything-but-trivial pursuit.

29. Most Valuable Player (MVP) Award

In 1910, Cleveland's Nap Lajoie and Detroit's Ty Cobb waged a battle of the bats in the American League to determine who would end the season with the highest average. The prize was a new Chalmers automobile. Confident of victory, Cobb quit the season early. Lajoie, however, boosted his average with seven bunts against St. Louis in the season's final games. Affable and easy going, Lajoie was well-liked among his fellow players, but the cantankerous, combative Cobb was not. American League president Ban Johnson suspected that the Cleveland and St. Louis players had conspired to help Lajoie and hurt Cobb. Although Cobb took the 1910 title, his and Lajoie's slugfest was so close that Chalmers ended up giving them both a car. The next year, the Chalmers company decided to base its award on a poll of sportswriters instead of player statistics. Cincinnati's Ren Mulford, a correspondent for *The Sporting Life*, agreed to select the first 12-man committee of sportswriters, and in 1911 they voted Cobb and Chicago's Wildfire Schulte as the American and National league MVPs. Although the Chalmers company expired long ago, the concept of writers selecting baseball's MVPs has endured ever since.

Twelve ways in which Ohio sports influenced the way we speak

> *"I had seen the first forward pass in football. It was illegal, of course."*
>
> —*John Heisman*

"HIKE"

Legendary coach and Cleveland native John Heisman was an amateur actor who instructed his players to call signals in "a cheerful, preppy tone." One of the snappy signals he coined was the word "hike," which quarterbacks still use to indicate the start of a play.

"PASSER AND RECEIVER"

If Notre Dame's Knute Rockne and Gus Dorais hadn't practiced the forward pass to near-perfection on the beach at Ohio's Cedar Point, the words passer and receiver might never have entered the lexicon. Curiously, Dorais used a baseball term—"pitcher"—to describe his role in the revolutionary football play, and Rockne likewise called himself the "catcher." But after the pair surprised Army and most of the world of sports with it in 1913, sportswriters started calling Dorais the "forward passer" and Rockne the "receiver."

"TAXI SQUAD"

Arthur "Mickey" McBride owned many businesses, including a taxicab company. When he started the Cleveland Browns in 1944, he gave the young players on the team's reserve list jobs driving his cabs. Pro football players who are under contract but not on the regular team have been called the taxi squad ever since.

"MIAMI OF OHIO"

This phrase is used by sports writers and broadcasters to distinguish Miami University in Oxford, Ohio, from the University of Miami, the Florida football factory that is big on winning big but considerably smaller on tradition.

"ACE"

This slang term for excellence can be traced to Asa Brainard, the pitcher of Cincinnati's undefeated 1869 Red Stockings. Thanks to him, the top pitcher was called an "asa" on baseball teams of the 1870s.

"FAN"

Derived from "fanatic," the word was first put into print by Cincinnati baseball writer Ren Mulford in *The Sporting News*, 1888.

"HOT STOVE LEAGUE"

The phrase was also coined by Ren Mulford, who used it to describe the baseball fans who frequently meet during the winter to talk about their favorite game.

"FIGHTING ILLINI"

When the University of Illinois played Ohio State in 1921, the game was a David-and-Goliath contest in which the Illini pulled off one of college football's classic upsets. The Buckeyes were undefeated, having blanked four other Big Ten schools by a total of 76 points. Illinois, on the other hand, had not only lost its four Big Ten games, but also not scored a single touchdown. When the two teams met at Ohio Field in Columbus, Ohio State should have had a cakewalk, but Illinois coach Bob Zuppke performed a minor gridiron miracle and beat John Wilce's Buckeyes, 7–0. The unexpected win over Ohio State inspired *Chicago Tribune* reporter Harvey Woodruff to call Zuppke's eleven the "Fighting Illini" in his column the next day, and the Illinois team has carried that proud nickname ever since.

"Annie Oakley"

The ace-of-hearts trick was one of the most popular feats that Darke County sharpshooter Annie Oakley performed in the late 1800s. With her husband holding the playing card, Annie took aim and neatly shot the heart out of the center. The stunt was such a crowd-pleaser that "Annie Oakley" became synonymous with pre-punched complimentary tickets. According to an apocryphal story, the phrase started after baseball czar Ban Johnson eyed a riddled ticket to a game and quipped, "That looks like Annie Oakley has been shooting at it."

"A Barney Oldfield"

The name of Wauseon native Berna Eli "Barney" Oldfield has become synonymous with reckless driving because of the speed demon reputation he earned as an auto racer in the early 1900s. Oldfield acquired a taste for speed during the bicycle craze of the Gay Nineties, then quickly graduated to motorcycles and automobiles. Henry Ford was building his first cars at the time, and in 1902, Oldfield signed on to drive one of them—the "999"—in a five-mile race against the auto everyone thought was too fast to be beaten: Alexander Winton's 50 miles-per-hour "Bullet." Oldfield left Winton in his dust, and the rush of publicity afterwards not only made his reputation as a race car driver, but also got Ford the investors he needed to start his motor company. The next year, Oldfield topped that feat and made himself a national hero when he took the "999" around a mile track in just over 59 seconds and became the first American to drive a gasoline-powered car a mile-a-minute. Cultivating his reckless image, Oldfield liked to be in the fast lane on and off the race track. He drank, smoked, frequented saloons, and, of course, made a lot of money quickly . . . only to spend it with equal speed.

"THANK YOU MRS. GRIFFIN"

The phrase became popular on bumper stickers in Columbus after Ohio State's 1974 season, when hometown football hero Archie Griffin not only won the Heisman Trophy, but also led the Buckeyes to defeat of archrival Michigan on their way to the Big Ten Championship and the Rose Bowl. Griffin was a slithery, bandy-legged Eastmoor High kid, and he had Heisman written all over him, from his freshman debut when he played briefly in the opening game against Iowa then against North Carolina, broke loose for 239 yards and the single-game school record.

"I just ran. That's all."

—*Archie Griffin, on his freshman debut*

Archie Griffin

PAUL BROWN
Football Coach and Innovator
Born: September 7, 1908, in Norwalk, Ohio
College: Miami University, 1930 (transferred from Ohio State, where his 140 pounds rendered him too small to play football)
Career: 1930–1931 Severn (Maryland) Preparatory School; 1932–1940 Massillon Washington High School (Massillon, Ohio); 1941–1943 Ohio State University; 1944–1945 Great Lakes Naval Training Station; 1946–1962 Cleveland Browns; 1968-1975 Cincinnati Bengals
Died: August 5, 1991, in Cincinnati

In 1946, when the new Cleveland football franchise held a contest to name the team, the most popular entry was "Browns." It was a telling tribute to the just-hired Paul Brown, whose stellar coaching records at both his hometown high school in Massillon and at Ohio State had already made him something of a football legend. Brown's Massillon Tigers took six consecutive state titles and were twice named U.S. scholastic champions, and in 1942, he led OSU to the national collegiate title in only his second year as the Buckeyes' coach. The magic continued from the 1940s through the 1950s, when Cleveland and "the Paul Brown System" dominated pro football with seven national championships. In 1968, Brown started a new team, the Cincinnati Bengals, whom he coached until retiring to their front office in 1975. After 41 years of coaching six teams, Brown had won .716 of his games. His innovative contributions to the game of football included the messenger playcall system, face guards on helmets, and putting players in classrooms, where Brown the Master Teacher even graded their playbooks. He crossed pro football's invisible color line by signing blacks, and his "alumni" comprise an all-star cast of the nation's coaches and players. Brown was inducted into the Pro Football Hall of Fame in 1967 and into the Ohio State University Hall Hall of Fame in 1991. In 1989, he was named the

Walter Camp Football Foundation's Man of the Year and selected for the National Football Foundation's Gold Medal, the highest honor awarded to an individual by that organization.

Little known fact: Brown is the only man in football who (1) took both college and NFL teams to national championships; (2) was the first coach of two teams; and (3) had a pro team named after him.

Paul Brown

"*We are all important but none of us are necessary.*"

— *Paul Brown*

A few words about him: "He was the greatest innovator the game of football has ever known. Halas football was grunt-and-groan sandlot football. Brown, with his offensive genius, brought the game into the modern era and has left a legacy that will perpetuate it." —Will McDonough, *The Boston Sunday Globe*

WAYNE WOODROW "WOODY" HAYES
Football Coach
Born: February 14, 1913, in Clifton, Ohio
College: Denison University, 1935
Career: 1935 Mingo Junction High School; 1936–1940 New Philadelphia High; 1946–1948 Denison University; 1949–1950 Miami University; 1951–1978 Ohio State University
Died: March 12, 1987, in Columbus

A writer once observed that Hayes sported a scarlet "O" cap for so many years that it seemed to be part of his head. It was meaningful observation, considering that before Hayes arrived, Ohio State's ardent, but acutely fickle fans had given the university a reputation for being a coaching graveyard. Hayes changed all that and lasted through 28 Ohio autumns because he did precisely what the people packing Ohio Stadium wanted: win football games. Between 1951 and 1978, Hayes had 205 wins, 10 ties, and only 61 losses. He took 13 Big Ten Conference titles and five national champions, coached 58 All-Americans, and won four Rose Bowls. When a game wasn't going his way, Hayes often peeled off his trademark cap and stomped on it. Some said his well-publicized tirades were mere theater; others saw the pure rage of a football perfectionist frustrated by an imperfect world. Though Hayes alternately cuffed his players and mother-henned them, he brought

Ohio State football into modern times with his top-notch recruits. Like his hero Billy Sherman (known to the rest of the world as General William Tecumseh), Hayes preferred a ground attack to the razzle-dazzle of taking to the air. His straightforward strategy worked beautifully in the golden years 1968–76, when he lost only 13 games and was the big fish in the Big Ten's exclusive pond. Hayes became one of the five winningest coaches in football, which to him was a metaphor for life. "Without winners, there can be no civilization," he wrote. But in his zeal to win, Hayes's behavior became too uncivilized to be politically correct, and finally, he slugged—on national television—a Clemson player during the

> *"I try not to be petty, but I am a petty person. And I have a terrible temper."*
>
> —*Woody Hayes*

Woody Hayes

67

1978 Gator Bowl. Hayes was never bitter about being fired, although it meant that his wish to die on the 50-yard line could never come true. He was elected to the College Football Hall of Fame in 1983, and in Columbus, he came to be regarded with the gentle affection reserved for patriarchs. When he died, flags flew at half-staff throughout the city.

Little known fact: Hayes was the first person to be named Coach of the Year three times—in 1957, 1968, and 1975— by the Football Writers of America.

A few words about him: "If Woody isn't a legend, he'll do until one comes along." —OSU Basketball coach Fred Taylor

JOHN HEISMAN
Football Coach and Pioneer
Born: October 23, 1869, in Cleveland
College: University of Pennsylvania, 1891 (transferred from Brown University)
Career: 1892 Oberlin College; 1893 Buchtel College (now University of Akron); 1894 Oberlin College; 1895 Auburn University; 1900–1903 Clemson University; 1904–1919 Georgia Institute of Technology; 1904–1919 University of Pennsylvania; 1923 Washington and Jefferson College; 1924–1927 Rice University
Died: October 3, 1936, in New York City

Heisman was a true pioneer of modern football. He lobbied for game quarters and the forward pass, taught his teams to start plays with voice signals; invented the snap from center, put downs and yards on the scoreboard, and developed the "Heisman shift," which was the granddaddy of the I and T formations. Heisman was a natural who earned one of the first football letters at Penn, but he cut his considerable coaching teeth at Ohio's Oberlin College, where his undefeated 1892 season was the springboard for his career. A trained actor with a gift for generating publicity, Heisman often sowed flowery phrases on the field of play, but his pretty words never belied his aggressive winning style. He was a disciplinarian who regarded breaking training rules to be tantamount to treason, and his players had to take cold showers after practice. Heisman expected his players to be talented, contentious, humble, smart, and swift, and his principles of football— e.g. "Always win the game. Never drop the ball."— are still

> *"Better to have died as a small boy than to fumble this football."*
>
> —*John Heisman*

John
Heisman

regarded as fundamentals of the game. When his coaching days were over, he went to New York City, where he became first president of the New York Touchdown Club and athletic director at the Downtown Athletic Club. The Heisman Memorial Trophy, which the Downtown Athletic Club annually awards to the nation's best college football player, is named in his honor. Heisman joined the College Football Hall of Fame in 1954.

Little known fact: In the most one-sided football game in history, Heisman coached Georgia Tech to a 222–0 win over Cumberland College of Tennessee, on October 7, 1916. The game had no first downs, because Cumberland never got one and Georgia Tech scored on every first set of downs. Although Georgia Tech also set records for the most touchdowns scored in a game (32) and was leading Cumberland 126–0 at halftime, Heisman urged his players to "hit 'em clean and hit 'em hard" in the second half, which is exactly what they did.

A few words about him: "He was a genius. He could take minimums and make them into maximums."—Georgia Tech center Al Loeb

KENESAW MOUNTAIN LANDIS
First Commissioner of Baseball
Born: November 20, 1866, in Millville, Ohio
College: Union Law School (now Northwestern University), 1891
Career: 1891–1905 attorney-at-law; 1905–1920 federal judge; 1921–1944 Commissioner of Baseball
Died: November 25, 1944, in Chicago

A product of the
Cincinnati YMCA
Law School,
Landis was
short-tempered,
arbitrary, and
often over-ruled.
The public liked
him anyway.
That, and a no-
cut contract from
baseball's owners,
made him the
most powerful
figure baseball
had ever seen.
His legacy
was the sport's
stability, and a
guarantee owners
would never see
anything like him
ever again.

—*The Cincinnati Game*

Kenesaw
Mountain Landis

"I never had any special desire to be a basketball player."

—Jerry Lucas

Landis never played in the major leagues or coached a team, yet he was arguably the most powerful figure that professional baseball has ever known. A lifelong fan, Landis had no formal association with baseball until 1921, when he became the presiding grand jury judge for eight Chicago White Sox players accused of throwing the 1919 World Series to the Cincinnati Reds. The once-idolized Chicago team was team was dubbed the "Black Sox," and the scandal seriously damaged the outraged public's perception of professional baseball's integrity. To restore the game's good name, the team owners sought out a man of sterling reputation as a singular baseball czar to replace baseball's faltering three-member ruling body. That man was Landis, who became the first Commissioner of Baseball in 1921 and soon served notice of his uncompromising intentions by imposing a life sentence of banishment from baseball on the Chicago Eight, even though a jury had acquitted them of fraud. For the next two decades, the granite-jawed Landis was the autocrat of baseball, guided by his own steadfast, prejudiced, and often arbitrary sense of what was good for the game. Landis opposed gambling, organized labor, the farm team system, and the integration of baseball, which he effectively blocked for two decades. He kicked a Phillies owner out of baseball for betting on his team, but looked the other way when Ty Cobb was accused of gambling on a game. Landis helped perpetuate the myth that Abner Doubleday invented baseball, but suspended the mythic Babe Ruth for barnstorming against his orders. Ironically, it was Ruth who served as Landis's unwittingly partner in salvaging baseball as the national pastime: Landis restored baseball's reputation, while the Sultan of Swat's relentless bat brought excitement—and fans—back to the games. Landis remained commissioner until his dying day and was inducted into Baseball Hall of Fame.

Little known fact: Landis's unusual first and middle names came from Kennesaw (spelled with two "n's") Mountain, Georgia, site of a Civil War battle that cost his father a leg.

A few words about him: "His career typifies the heights to which dramatic talent may carry a man in America, if only he has the foresight not to go on stage." —Heywood Hale Broun

JERRY LUCAS
Basketball Player
Born: March 30, 1940, in Middletown, Ohio
College: The Ohio State University, 1962
Career: 1960–1962 The Ohio State University; 1963–1969 Cincinnati Royals; 1969–1971 San Francisco Warriors; 1971–1974 New York Knicks

Lucas is one of only a handful of American athletes—and certainly the first basketball player—to attain championships at every level of play: high school, college, Olympic, and professional. The superb Lucas saga began at Middletown High in the late 1950s, where he was, in today's descriptive parlance, a 6' 8" phenom. Lucas piled up 2,446 points; led the Middies to not only two consecutive state championships (1956, 1957), but also a 76-game winning streak that set a national record; and established his still-unbroken state record for the most points scored by a player—56—in an Ohio high school tournament. Lucas, of course, became one of the most heavily recruited prep players in the nation, but he decided on Ohio State during a fishing trip, when basketball coach Fred Taylor lured him to Columbus with the promise of a good education. Lucas became the Buckeyes' all-time top scorer, accumulating 1,990 points, for an average of 23.4 per game. He topped the nation in field goals three years in a row, and his .624 career

Jerry Lucas, a 6' 8" prep phenom—he was that tall at 15—established his greatness before he entered Middletown High. On the town's outdoor courts, Lucas squared off against 6' 8" Johnny Horan, twice MVP at the University of Dayton, and ate his considerable lunch. Asked Horan afterward: "What year is that guy?"

Answer: "He's a freshman."

Horan: "What college?"

Answer: "Junior High."

field goal percentage is still an Ohio State record. As college basketball's only three-time Big Ten Player of the Year, Lucas was also a three-time All-American and two-time National Player of the Year. Always a "team player" in the finest sense of the phrase, Lucas hooked up with John Havlicek to steer the Buckeyes to the 1960 national collegiate championship and to consecutive runner-up spots in 1961 and 1962. Lucas, along with Oscar Robertson, also starred on the first U.S. Olympic "Dream Team," which brought home the gold in 1960. After Ohio State, Lucas turned pro and signed with the Royals, where he averaged 17.7 points a game and was the National Basketball Association Rookie of the Year. He also became one of only two men in NBA history—the other was the prodigious Wilt Chamberlain—to average 20 points and 20 rebounds in two consecutive seasons. Lucas crowned his career in 1973, when he was a center on the Knicks team that won the NBA championship.

Little known fact: Always a serious student, Lucas went to OSU on an academic, not athletic, scholarship and became an honor student. He now creates educational materials and lectures on memory improvement. His own memory is so sharp that he once learned the New Testament and the first 20 pages of the Manhattan telephone book by heart.

A few words about him: "He's the greatest player I ever coached."—1960 Olympic basketball coach Fred Newell

JACK NICKLAUS
Professional Golfer
Born: January 21, 1940, in Columbus
College: The Ohio State University, 1957–1962, and an honorary Doctorate of Athletic Arts, 1972

Career: 1959 U.S. Amateur; 1961 U.S. Amateur; 1962 U.S. Open; 1963 Masters, PGA; 1964 Australian Open; 1965 Masters; 1966 Masters, British Open; 1967 U.S. Open; 1968 Australian Open; 1970 British Open; 1971 PGA, Australian Open; 1972 U.S. Open, Masters; 1973 PGA; 1975 PGA, Masters, Australian Open; 1976 Australian Open; 1978 British Open, Australian Open; 1980 U.S. Open, PGA; 1986 Masters; 1991 PGA Seniors, U.S. Senior Open

When he won the U.S. Open in 1962, Nicklaus was only 22, the youngest golf champion in nearly four decades. They put a picture of the blond, burly "Golden Bear" on the cover of Time. Not bad for a kid from Columbus with the dew from the links at Ohio State still fresh on his clubs. Nicklaus not only began to topple America's reigning golf king Arnold Palmer, but also sent "Arnie's Army" of fans into retreat. With his concentration, accuracy, and powerful swing, Nicklaus dominated golf for a quarter of a century. A five-time Professional Golf Association Player of the Year (1967, 1972, 1973, 1975, and 1976), he holds the record for winning the most major championships (20); is the only man to win the five major tournaments—U.S. Open, Masters, PGA, U.S. Amateur, British Open—twice; and has career earnings exceeding $6 million. He was declared the PGA's Golfer of the Century in 1988. The Bear has mellowed with the years and no longer competes as often on golf courses, preferring instead to design his own world class "signature" courses. Still, Nicklaus's endurance remains his most impressive record. In 1963, when he won his first Masters tournament, he set a record for being the youngest person—age 23—ever to win it. In 1986, when he won the Masters for a record-setting sixth time, he was 46 and the oldest golf champion of any decade. With that win, the incomparable Nicklaus put his true signature on the mantle of Time.

"I was 13, working in the drugstore with my father. We slipped away to play nine holes before dinner, and I had 35 on the front nine. I begged him to go on. No, he said. Mom had dinner cooking. But if we ate fast . . . we could be back in 35 minutes. Later, needing an eagle on the last hole for 69, I. . .made a long rainbow putt. I think that's when my father decided I had a better future as a golfer than as a stock boy."

—Jack Nicklaus, on the first time he broke 70

> *"It's hard not to play golf that's up to Jack Nicklaus' standards when you are Jack Nicklaus."*
>
> —*Jack Nicklaus*

Little known fact: Under the tutelage of his father, Charles Nicklaus, he played his first round at age ten, scoring 51 on 9 holes. Fifteen years later, he set a record for the lowest 72-hole total—271—at the Masters tournament.

A few words about him: "He's just better than the rest of us. I think it's in his genes. He's the greatest player who ever lived. He was better than us back then, and he's better now."— Chi Chi Rodriguez

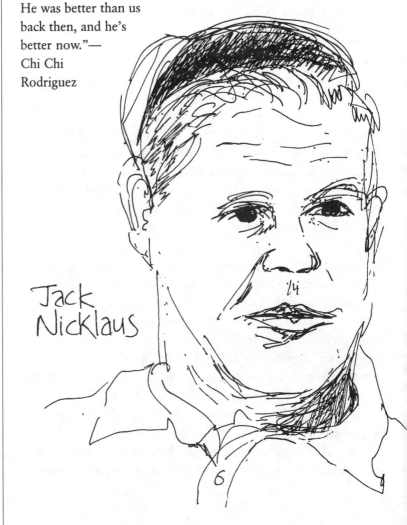

Jack Nicklaus

ANNIE OAKLEY

Sharpshooter/Entertainer
Born: August 13, 1860, on a farm near Greenville
College: None
Career: 1875–1885 performed in vaudeville and circuses
with husband Frank Butler; 1885–1901 starred in Buffalo Bill
Cody's touring Wild West Show; 1902–1922 competed
in shooting matches and exhibitions; shooting instructor
at Pinehurst, North Carolina, resort hotel; entertained
World War I troops
Died: November 2, 1926, in Greenville

Annie Oakley wielded rifles, shotguns, and pistols with the
same ease that other Victorian women used with their knitting
needles. She could shatter two swinging balls with a single shot
and shoot the flames off candles mounted on a rotating wheel.
She could have two clay pigeons released from traps, run 20
feet, vault over a table, pick up a gun, take aim, and still pick
off both targets in mid-air. Born Phoebe Anne Moses to a poor
Darke County farm family, Oakley learned to take aim as a
child in order to put game on the table. It was a harsh life, and
she literally shot her way out of threadbare obscurity and into
the limelight. By the time Oakley turned 20, she was a professional exhibition shooter, and her skill with firearms would win
her a devoted husband, fortune, fame, and ultimately immor-
tality as the subject of the musical *Annie Get Your Gun*. Oakley
was a superb athlete and actress. As the headliner in the
phenomenally popular Wild West Show, she turned cartwheels
and did handsprings and jumped on and off galloping horses,
all the while firing her name, reputation, and legend into the
collective conscious of millions of people. Pretty and petite, she
was a feminine fantasy in fringe and buckskin who brandished
one of the strongest symbols of masculinity, and audiences
loved the anomaly of a woman with a weapon. Sitting Bull

*"If my aim had
been poorer, I
might have
averted the Great
War."*

—*Annie Oakley, on putting
Kaiser Wilhelm
into her act*

77

made her his adopted daughter; Queen Victoria called her a "very clever little girl;" and Germany's Crown Prince Wilhelm had her shoot a lighted cigarette out of his lips. Before, during, and after her years of entertaining in the Wild West, Oakley the *precision* shooter competed in matches for pay and prizes. She once pocketed $9,000 from just one tournament in England, and Oakley collected more than $100,000 worth of trophies during her career. In 1922, she celebrated her 62nd birthday by shooting a hundred clay pigeons in a row. By her own account, Oakley fired a least one million shells during her lifetime, and almost all of them were right on target.

A few words about her:"Miss Oakley is lithe and slender, and when her figure is poised in the act of aiming at an object, she is decidedly charming, but the sharp retort of the rifle breaks the spell, and the contemplation of the pretty girl gives place to admiration of her phenomenal skill. Her aim seems to be simply unerring."—*Patterson Daily Guardian*, 1889

BRANCH RICKEY
Baseball Coach, Manager, and Executive
Born: December 20, 1881, in Stockdale, Pike County
College: Ohio Wesleyan University, 1906; University of Michigan law, 1911
Career: 1913–1916 St. Louis Browns; 1917–1942 St. Louis Cardinals; 1942–1950 Brooklyn Dodgers; 1950–1960 Pittsburgh Pirates
Died: December 9, 1965, in Columbia, Missouri

Rickey's talent for finding and developing good ball players was the particular genius with which he founded three baseball dynasties. Rickey was born in the hardscrabble southern Ohio hill country to a farm couple who eventually moved to Lucasville, where their bright young son could enjoy the advantages of a town school. From his athletic father, Rickey inherited the genes that put him on Ohio Wesleyan's baseball team, and from his Scripture-reading mother, he got the philosophy that kept him off the diamond on Sundays. When tuberculosis interrupted his playing career and hard times undermined his law practice, Rickey turned to major league baseball, becoming a scout, manager, and finally executive. Players knew him as shrewd and something of a skinflint, but if Rickey ran his teams with an iron hand in a leather glove, he was also considered fair-minded. His decidedly practical leadership of the St. Louis Cardinals, Brooklyn Dodgers, and Pittsburgh Pirates made powerhouses and pennant winners of them all. Along the way, Rickey signed more than a few baseball greats—Campanella, Clemente, Newcombe, Sisler— and he made two innovations that changed the game forever: the farm team in 1919, and racial integration in 1947. Since the Cardinals couldn't afford to hire major talents, Rickey "grew" them in minor league teams, and he broke major league baseball's long ban on black players by signing Jackie Robinson to the Dodgers. It is said that Rickey waited 40 years to find the right man with the intelligence and moral courage to successfully integrate baseball. His landmark decision not only strengthened baseball, but also ultimately the country by calling attention to the national hypocrisy about civil rights. After his Pittsburgh Pirates won the World Series in 1960, Rickey tried to form a new Continental League, an ill-fated effort that nonetheless resulted in the major leagues expanding. He was inducted into the Baseball Hall of Fame in 1967.

Little known fact: Born into a very religious Methodist family, Rickey called the notebook where he tracked potential players, the "Bible."

"Thou shalt not steal. I mean defensively. On offense, indeed thou shalt steal and thou must."
—*Branch Rickey*

A few words about him: "Rickey was a man who worked, schemed, and connived to build winning teams simply for the sake of being associated with a winner."—Daniel Okrent and Harris Lewine, *The Ultimate Baseball Book*

PETE ROSE
Baseball Player and Manager
Born: April 14, 1942, in Cincinnati
College: none
Career: 1963–1978 Cincinnati Reds; 1979–1983 Philadelphia Phillies; 1984 Montreal Expos, Cincinnati Reds (player/manager); 1985–1987 Cincinnati Reds (player/manager); 1987–1989 Cincinnati Reds (manager)

His pinnacle came in Cincinnati on September 11, 1985, when Rose, on the 57th anniversary of Ty Cobb's last game, surpassed Cobb's 4,191 base hits, thus breaking the record that conventional sports wisdom said could never be broken. Rose—in his hometown, at the overripe age of 44, playing for the Reds with whom he had

*"Sure, I know I
make more
money than the
President of the
United States,
but he can't hit
a slider."*

—Pete Rose

Pete Rose

begun his major league career 23 years before—had not only defied the odds, but also elevated himself to the small pantheon of baseball deities via his sheer, unabashed love of the game of baseball. Whatever the thorns in his personal life, Rose wore both his heart and soul on his uniform sleeve, achieving a giddy status in the litany of baseball mosts—career hits (4,256), at-bats (14,053), games (3,562), winning games, singles (3,215), and seasons with 200 or more hits. He is also the only man in baseball to have played 500 games at five positions—first, second, and third base; right and left field. Rose the Player became Rose the Manager in 1986, but not before he tacked another 64 base hits onto his record, thus insuring a long haul for any would-be equal with a bat. The lifelong goal of this perpetual Boy of Summer was, of course, the Baseball Hall of Fame, and his remarkable record should have made his selection a given. But Rose was shut out on August 23, 1989, when the commissioner of baseball banned him from the game for life after a scandal over his betting on baseball games. Rose also spent five months in a federal prison for underreporting his income to the Internal Revenue Service. After his 1991 release, he moved to Florida and now devotes his time to broadcasting and business interests.

Little known fact: In 1978, Rose not only set a National League hitting streak record of 44 consecutive games, but also became only the 13th major league player to get 3,000 career hits.

A few words about him: "Pete got his hits the way he got everything—through scrap, hustle, aggressiveness, alertness, and running like the wind. If DiMaggio was a sleek 747, Pete was a World War I bi-plane, held together with chewing gum and piano wire."—sports writer Jim Murray

DENTON TRUE "CY" YOUNG
Pitcher
Born: March 29, 1867, in Gilmore, Tuscarawas County
College: none
Career: 1890–1898 Cleveland Spiders; 1899–1900 St. Louis
Cardinals; 1901–1908 Boston Red Sox; 1909–1911 Cleveland
Naps; 1912 Boston Braves (incomplete season)
Died: November 4, 1955, near Newcomerstown,
Tuscarawas County

Young received his middle name of True from the surname of a
soldier who saved his father's life in the Civil War, but he got
his nickname in Canton, where he threw baseballs with such
velocity into the ballpark fence that folks said it reminded them
of a cyclone. Thus, "Cy" Young began to carve out his incomparable place on the baseball mound. His strength and size—
Young was 6' 2" and weighed 210 pounds as a teenager—came
from hard work as a farmer and rail-splitter back in Tuscarawas
County. Young always took pride in the fact he never had a
sore arm in his baseball career, and he credited his off-season
farm chores with keeping his muscles in shape. In his first
major league season, Young pitched—and won—a doubleheader that demonstrated his great control and signaled his
future greatness. He played in the first forerunner of the World
Series (1903, with the winning Red Sox); pitched three no-hit,
no-run games as well as the twentieth century's first perfect
game (1904); and set a record for the most games pitched
(906) that was not broken until 1968. Though Young quit
baseball in 1912, he remains the only pitcher to win 200 games
in both the National and American Leagues, and three of his
lifetime pitching records still stand: most wins (511), most
completed games (751), and most innings pitched (7,377).
Of course, he was a shoo-in for the Baseball Hall of Fame, and

> "Cy Young and his sister have still got them all beat."
>
> —Roger Angell,
> on argument as
> to whom was greatest
> set of sibling pitchers

Cy Young

the annual Cy Young Award, which is given to baseball's best
pitcher, fittingly bears the name of the Ohioan who set the
standard for generations of pitchers. Young spent much
of his major league career in Cleveland, and upon retiring his
splendid arm at age 45, he returned home to the farms
of Tuscarawas County, where he worked the land until he
was in his eighties.

Little known fact: After Cy Young left the mound and went
back to Tuscarawas County, he got so many letters from
admirers that the government kept the tiny post office
in Peoli open primarily to handle his fan mail.

A few words about him:

> *Y is for Young*
>
> *The Magnificent Cy;*
>
> *People batted against him,*
>
> *But I never knew why.*
>
> *—Ogden Nash*

"FATHER FOOTBALL"—Paul Brown, football's all-time innovator, who coached Ohio State to the 1942 national college title and took the Cleveland Browns to four consecutive All-America Football Conference championships (1946, 1947, 1948, and 1949) and three National Football League championships (1950, 1954, and 1955).

"ROGER THE DODGER"—Roger Staubach, the Cincinnati native and nimble Dallas Cowboys quarterback of the 1970s, whose scrambling footwork gave him 20 rushing touchdowns, and 2,264 rushing yards, in addition to his 22,700 throwing yards.

"FLAT-FOOT FRANKIE"/"FIREBALL FRANKIE"—Youngstown's Frank Sinkwich, the Heisman Trophy winner with the sore, but swift feet who in the 1943 Rose Bowl scored the only touchdown in Georgia's 9–0 victory over UCLA.

"THE TOE"—Martins Ferry native and impeccable place kicker and offensive tackle Lou Groza, who spent his entire career with the Cleveland Browns. In 21 seasons between 1946 and 1967, he scored 1,349 points, a tally that places him ninth on the NFL's list of all-time leading scorers. Only six of those points were from a touchdown; the rest came from post-touchdown extra points and field goals. His most famous footwork was the field goal that gave the Browns their first NFL title in the final seconds of the 1950 championship game, when they beat the Rams 30–28.

"GLUE FINGERS"—Hudson native Dante Lavelli, the sure-handed Cleveland Browns receiver who was quarterback Otto Graham's favorite target in the 1940s and 1950s.

"LENNY THE COOL"—Alliance native and Kansas City's chief quarterback for 14 seasons Len Dawson, who was known for his poise and passing accuracy. His early years with the Steelers and Browns were lackluster. But after joining Kansas City in 1963, his accurate arm and play calling took the team to Super Bowl I, where Dawson got the ignominy of being the event's first losing quarterback, and to Super Bowl IV, where he redeemed himself as the Most Valuable Player when the Chiefs conquered the Vikings 23–7.

"THE POPE"—Chuck Noll, the future Football Hall of Fame coach whose University of Dayton education apparently made him an exceptionally smart pupil of Paul Brown when he played guard for Cleveland in the 1950s.

"KARDIAC KIDS"—the Cleveland Browns team of 1979–1980, which was coached by Sam Rutigliano and led by the cool-headed, confident quarterback Brian Sipe to a succession of come-from-behind wins that earned them the 1980 American Football Conference Central Division title.

"GRAVEYARD OF COACHES"—Ohio State University, which before the Woody Hayes era began in 1951 had five coaches in 11 years, including Francis Schmidt, Carroll Widdoes, Paul Bixler, and Wes Fesler.

"HACKSAW"—Jack Reynolds, whom students of the NFL remember as the linebacker who made the third quarter tackle that gave San Francisco the winning edge over Cincinnati in the 1982 Super Bowl. Born and raised in Cincinnati, Reynolds got his nickname not from his tackles but his temper. When his team at the University of Tennessee was denied a Sugar Bowl bid by Ole Miss in 1969, Reynolds took his frustration out on a junked Chevy: he bought a box of hacksaws and cut the car in half.

> *" A local sports-writer called me and said, 'You've been drafted. What's your reaction?'*
> *I thought he meant into the Army because the Korean War was in progress..."*
>
> —*Chuck Noll, on being drafted by the Cleveland Browns in 1953*

> *"If you never saw Chic Harley run with a football, we obviously could not describe it for you. It wasn't like Grange or Harmon or anybody else. It was kind of a cross between music and cannon fire, and it brought your heart up under your ears."*
>
> —*James Thurber*

"HOPALONG CASSADY"—Howard Cassady, the 1950s Ohio State Heisman Trophy winner, whose surname and habit of jumping over the line when he ran inspired sportswriters to tag him with the nickname of another popular Ohioan, television cowboy star Hopalong Cassidy.

"BOXCAR BAILEY"—James Bailey, the legendary Hamilton High fullback who hit football foes like a locomotive and starred at Miami University in 1950, when he delivered sure-footed winning performances in both the snowbound Cincinnati game and subsequent Salad Bowl.

"THE IMMORTAL CHIC"—Charles "Chic" Harley, who transformed football from a run-of-the-mill sport to a way of life at Ohio State. As the Buckeye's first three-time All-American (1916, 1917, and 1919), the unassuming, boyish-looking halfback was Ohio State's first superstar, scoring 203 points in 23 games. Harley was adept at the pass, punt, and dropkick, but it was his crowd-pleasing, cat-like runs that catapulted Ohio State into a Big Ten football power and nationally known team.

"CITY OF CHAMPIONS"—Massillon, which is arguably the most football-minded town in Ohio and the place where the high school booster club gives baby boys a football just after they're born. Its pigskin pride springs from Massillon Washington High, where legendary coach Paul Brown launched a football program that took him to the college and pro ranks and took the school to 17 state championships between 1940 and 1980. On September 13, 1985, the Tigers also claimed the distinction of being the first football team in the nation to win 600 games. All told, the school has won 22 state championships and nine national championships; had 20 undefeated seasons and another 20 with only one loss; and

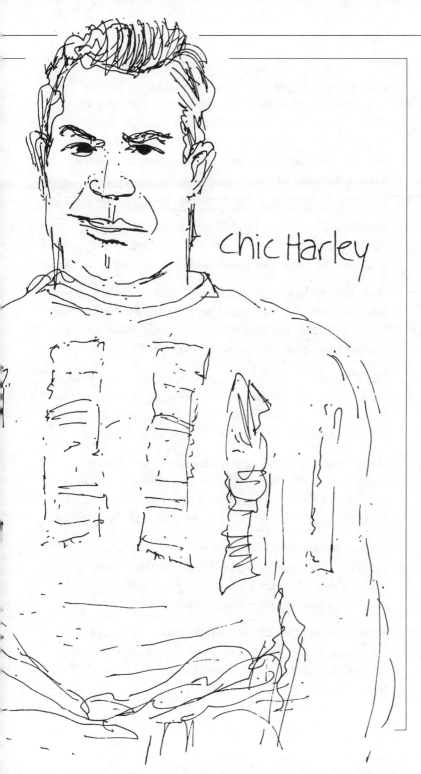

Chic Harley

All-American Chic Harley never played in a losing game his first two years. Even when he left for military service in World War I, he was on the winning side. When Harley returned to OSU for the 1919 season, it looked as if the Buckeyes would go undefeated again. But in the last ten seconds of the last game, when Illinois kicked a field goal to win, he found himself on the losing team for the first time in his college career.

"A man opposed to Sunday baseball except when the gate receipts exceeded $5,000."

—*John Lardner on Branch Rickey*

produced more than 35 All-Americans and pro players. Massillon alumni include All-Pro players Robert Vogel and Tommy James, as well as coaches Earle Bruce (Ohio State), Bob Commings (Iowa), Leo Strang (Kent State), Lee Tressel (Baldwin-Wallace), Don James (Washington), and Chuck Mather (Chicago Bears).

"THE MASSILLON MISSILE"—Chris Spielman, the honor student and linebacker from Massillon who became an All-American at Ohio State, won the Lombardi trophy in 1987, and made All-Pro with the Detroit Lions.

"MR. BASEBALL"—Branch Rickey, the Pike County native who, as a player, manager, and general manager, spent 59 years of his life in baseball, during which he made Jackie Robinson the first black player in the major leagues.

"EL CHEAPO"—Branch Rickey again, whose purse strings were so tightly pulled that when Enos Slaughter tried out for the Cardinals in 1934, Rickey told Slaughter that if he didn't make the team, he'd have to pay his own travel expenses.

"DUKE OF TRALEE"—the totally mythological moniker applied to Baseball Hall of Famer Roger Bresnahan, a native of Toledo, who often feigned Irish origin as a catcher for New York, St. Louis, Chicago, and other teams in the early 1900s.

"ROUGHHOUSE REDS"—manager Chuck Dressen's Cincinnati Reds team of 1934–37, whose three losing seasons explains why they were known for the aggressiveness of their style rather than the substance of their play.

"THE BIG RED MACHINE"—the smooth, sharp, splendid Cincinnati Reds of the 1970s, a well-oiled team that made winning the World Series back-to-back in 1975 and 1976 look almost effortless.

"SLOWEST MAN IN BASEBALL"—Cincinnati Reds catcher Ernie Lombardi, who earned his slowly reputation in the 1930s and 1940s, when he was almost as famous for dragging his feet as he was for wielding his league-leading bat. Although he played in more than 1800 major league games, he stole a total of only eight bases during his career.

"THE BIG SLUG" AND "THE LITTLE SLUG"—the dynamic catching duo of Ernie Lombardi and his back-up, Willard Hershberger, who got his lackadaisical sobriquet by association with the Reds' slow starter.

"BIG KLU"—Ted Kluszewski, the gentle giant and popular Cincinnati power hitter in the 1950s, who had developed his huge biceps by carrying heavy sacks in a cornstarch mill. A Reds first baseman from 1947–1957, the 6' 2", 240–pound Kluszewski led the major leagues in 1954 with 49 home runs and 141 runs batted in, and he was a National League All-Star from 1953–1956.

"CHARLIE HUSTLE"—the fitting nickname that Mickey Mantle pinned on Pete Rose, who was arguably the most enthusiastic and determined player the Reds, if not baseball, ever knew.

"CAPTAIN HOOK"—Cincinnati Reds manager George Lee "Sparky" Anderson, the phenomenal strategist who led the team to four National League and two World Series championships in the 1970s and was known for his habit of yanking faltering pitchers out of games.

"THE COBRA"—Cincinnati's Dave Parker, the hometown hitter with the snake-like swing whose batting average, home runs, and RBIs led the Reds in 1984 and 1985.

"How hard is hitting? You ever walk into a pitch-black room full of furniture that you've never been in before and try to walk through without bumping into anything? Well, it's harder than that."

—Ted Kluszewski

> *"And so they escorted her off the field, two a breast."*
>
> —*Si Burick, Dayton Daily News sportswriter, on Morganna's removal from a game*

"NASTY BOYS"—1990 Cincinnati Reds pitchers Norm Charlton, Rob Dibble, and Randy Myers, a bullpen trio armed with evil 90–100 mile per hour fast balls that were bad news for opposing hitters.

"KISSING BANDIT"—Morganna Roberts, the blonde and bold exotic dancer from Columbus whose sideline is bussing unsuspecting ballplayers in the middle of their games.

"RAPID ROBERT"—Bob Feller, the right-handed Cleveland pitcher who once threw the swiftest fast ball—98.6 mph—in baseball. In 1936 at age 17, Feller became the youngest player the Indians have ever had. He spent his entire career with the tribe and superbly spanned the mid-1930s to mid-1950s: winning 20 or more games in a season six times; leading the league multiple times in wins, strikeouts, and innings pitched; stacking up 266 career wins; and throwing 12 one-hitters and three no-hitters, one of which (April 16, 1940) was major league baseball's first and only such feat on opening day.

"TRADER LANE"—Cleveland Indians general manager Frank Lane, who between December, 1957, and December, 1959, made 60 separate player deals, including the disastrous trade of the enormously popular home run champ Rocky Colavito for Harvey Kueen.

♦ **"BIG O"**—Oscar Robertson, who took his all-black high school back home in Indiana to two state championships, but refined his winning ways at the University of Cincinnati. In 1958, he not only became the first sophomore ever named college player of the year, but also repeated the honor as a junior and senior. Robertson was co-captain of the U.S. team that brought home a gold medal from the 1960 Olympics. He then had ten superlative years of shooting and playmaking with the Cincinnati Royals and four more with the Milwaukee Bucks, where he played "Mr. Outside" to "Mr. Inside," Lew

Alcindor (a.k.a. Kareem Abdul-Jabbar). A versatile, all-around player and playmaker, Robertson was on every All-Star team between 1961 and 1969. His 26,710 career points and 9,887 assists put him, respectively, fifth and second on the National Basketball Association's all-time lists.

"HONDO"—Martins Ferry native John Havlicek, who was an all-Ohio quarterback at Bridgeport High School then played football as well as basketball at Ohio State, where he was a member of the legendary 1960 team that won the NCAA's college basketball crown. Drafted by both the Cleveland Browns and Boston Celtics in 1962, he stayed with basketball and spent 16 years as the Celtics' "sixth man," shifting effortlessly from forward to guard as the team rolled to eight NBA championships. In 1974, Havlicek became the eighth player in pro basketball history to score 20,000 career points. All told, he played in 1270 regular season games and racked up 26,395 points, the sixth highest tally in NBA history.

"THE GENERAL"—Orrville's Bobby Knight, the volatile University of Indiana basketball coach known for blowing his top and his cool, but not his games. Knight has a better-than-.700 record of career wins. His Indiana teams took NCAA championships in 1976, 1981, and 1987, and he coached the U.S. Olympic team to a gold medal in 1984.

"THE DRAGON"—Bobby Knight again, who as a substitute player on the smoking OSU teams of the early 1960s, got the nickname not from breathing fire on the basketball court, but because he duped folks into believing he belonged to a motorcycle gang called the Dragons.

"CARNAK THE GREAT"—Jack Nicklaus, who was given the nickname—a take-off on Johnny Carson's old late night television routine—by his professional golf colleagues because of his discourses on the game.

♦ *Cincinnati resident Oscar Robertson's uniform number has been retired by two NBA teams—No. 1, by Milwaukee, and No. 14, by Sacramento*

DAN REEVES VS. CLEVELAND

Cleveland Rams owner Reeves astounded the city of Cleveland and most of the National Football League on January 14, 1946, when he announced that he was moving the Rams from Cleveland to Los Angeles. The Rams had just won the 1945 NFL championship by beating the Washington Redskins 15–14 in Cleveland Stadium. Reeves was peeved because only about 32,000 people turned out to witness the home team victory. Adding injury to insult, the city had not only tripled the rent on Cleveland Stadium for the game, but the financially troubled Rams' receipts were also being threatened by a new pro team coming to town, the Cleveland Browns. Reeves's bitter departure was risky business, because at that time there were no other pro football teams in California, commercial air travel was in its infancy, and the nearest city with a football franchise was 2,000 miles away. But his quarrel with Cleveland paid off handsomely in Los Angeles. Reeves signed big name players and the winning Rams attracted huge crowds, a resounding success that started the spread of pro sports to the West Coast.

ART MODELL VS. PAUL BROWN

In 1961, Modell, a young New York television and advertising mogul, bought controlling interest of the Cleveland Browns for an unheard-of $4 million. The deal, of course, included Paul Brown, a seasoned football legend who was not only the team's namesake, but also the Coach with a capital C whose command of the team resulted in four All-America Football Conference titles and three National Football League championships between 1946 and 1955. Almost immediately, Modell riled Brown by taking a personal interest in the team's management and players. The two clashed, and after grumblings about Brown's coaching style from some veteran players, Modell fired him early in 1963, reportedly saying, "This team won't be mine until you're not around." Brown later took his shot at Modell, when he described their rift as "a basic conflict between two different philosophies of operating—one from knowledge and experience; the other from a complete lack of either." The firing got banner headlines, and outraged Browns fans directed their wrath at Modell. Fathers even handed this animosity down to their sons, so that by the time Brown died in 1991, there was a second generation of Clevelanders resenting Modell for the pink slip he had issued nearly thirty years before. Brown, of course, had his detractors, who

"When you lose, say little. When you win, say less."

—*Paul Brown*

95

> *"Arnie created golf. Jack perfected it."*
>
> —*Paul Daugherty*

claimed that time—and the game—had passed the aging coach by. But when Cleveland took the NFL title in 1964, Brown's supporters noted that Modell got the championship with the former coach's players. After his dismissal, Brown's contract kept him on the team's payroll for a few more years, and in the "darkest period" of his life, the old coach cooled his heels and itched for an opportunity to get back into football. It came in 1967, when the American Football League was expanding and awarding franchises. Thanks to Modell, Brown was ready, willing, and available to return to football, which he did grandly by starting a new pro team—the Cincinnati Bengals—that he could both coach and control. His Bengals got off to a roaring start: by 1969, Brown was named AFL Coach of the Year, and at the end of only their third season, the Bengals were the American Football Conference Central Division champs. Cleveland's loss had turned out to be Cincinnati's gain.

JACK NICKLAUS VS. ARNOLD PALMER

The two most dominant and visible figures in golf during the last half of the twentieth century, Nicklaus and Palmer share remarkably common ground. Both learned the game that would bring them wealth and fame from their fathers. As a pre-schooler, Palmer moved to Latrobe, Pennsylvania, where his father was the country club pro, and he made a name for himself on the professional links in the late 1950s and 1960s. It was the heyday of television, and Palmer was the perfect golfer for television—affable, attractive, and an expert at executing nail-biting, come-from-behind birdies that won tournaments and kept viewers glued to their easy chairs. He attracted a veritable army of admirers, and his claim to the kingdom of modern golf might have gone unchallenged were it not for the Young Turk Nicklaus nipping at his throne. Although Nicklaus was only 14 when he first sized up Palmer at the Ohio amateur championship, the defining moment in their relationship came in 1962, when the 22-year-old Nicklaus beat Palmer in his own backyard for the U.S. Open title at Pittsburgh's Oakmont Country Club. They continued to battle each other on the greens and on television, but within a decade, Nicklaus's brilliant string of major tournament victories in the 1960s and 1970s eclipsed Palmer's career. In truth, Nicklaus picked up where Palmer left off: Palmer ushered in the era of golf as a spectator sport and television entertainment, but the phenomenal Nicklaus brought it to unprecedented popularity in both areas. An unheard-of nine million people had tuned in to watch their fateful playoff in Pittsburgh, and the golf that they played before the masses made them both rich. In 1967, Palmer became the first golfer to earn $1 million; in 1988, Nicklaus was the first to earn $5 million. As Palmer bowed out of the PGA tour and Nicklaus continued to compete, their gentlemanly, but keen competition shifted from prize money to business. Both shrewdly went after golf clothing, equipment, and other endorsements, and both designed "signature" golf courses.

CLEVELAND BROWNS VS. CINCINNATI BENGALS

The Battle of Ohio rages twice each season when the state's professional football foes meet in Cleveland and Cincinnati. As rivalries go, theirs is a relatively new one, for it began after the National Football League merged with the American Football League following the 1969 season. Existing teams were realigned into two NFL conferences, with the old NFL's Browns and the AFL's Bengals both placed in the American Football Conference's Central Division. When the Browns met the Bengals for the first time in a 1970 exhibition game in Cincinnati, the cross-state clash carried not only the vestiges of the old NFL-AFL rivalry, but also the personal baggage of the still-fresh 1960s rift between Browns owner Art Modell and Bengals boss Paul Brown. When the Browns and the Bengals took the field before a standing-room-only crowd, their highly similar orange-and-brown uniforms were an obvious indication of their highly similar origins, for both had been founded and formed in the image of Paul Brown. The Bengals beat the Browns in that first exhibition 31–24, but in regular play from 1970 through their mutually dismal 1993 seasons, the teams have been almost evenly matched in their series, with the Bengals winning 24 games and the Browns 23. In that same period, the Bengals have appeared in—and lost—two Super Bowls, but the Browns, alas, have been to none. Brown's death in 1991 finally removed the personal factor from the Browns-Bengals rivalry, which has become yet another point of contention in the ongoing municipal tug-of-war between Cleveland and Cincinnati. For years, the brawny, industrial city-state on Lake Erie and the Ohio River city with its genteel Southern exposure have feuded over which is bigger, better, classier, and more cultured. Thus, residents in both cities regard the

score of the Browns-Bengals games to be a matter of civic pride, if not chauvinism. Cincinnati and Cleveland mayors have even been known to wager, respectively, a pot of Cincinnati chili and a batch of kielbasa sausages on a game's outcome. In 1986, Cincinnati Mayor Charles Luken said he would fly Cleveland's flag over City Hall if the Bengals lost. They suffered a 34-3 shellacking from the Browns, and Luken kept his word, but not until December 21. It's the shortest day of the year, and the mayor wanted Cincinnati's embarrass-ment to be as brief as possible.

"They are up there, the huddled, sooty masses on their frozen, Rust Belt tundra, living their pitiful Cleveland lives."

—*Cincinnati columnist Paul Daugherty, on Cleveland fans*

"So universal is football daffiness in the region that during the recent political campaign, one canard circulated about a candidate had it that his entire foreign policy could be summed up in two words: 'Beat Michigan!' "

—John McNulty
on OSU football

OHIO STATE VS. UNIVERSITY OF MICHIGAN

The University of Michigan's football media guide has declared the annual contest between the Ohio State Buckeyes and the Wolverines "The Big Game, College Football's Greatest Rivalry." Autumnal hype aside, it may well be just that: an impassioned, emotionally charged meeting with the pride of two universities and two next-door states resting precariously on the final score. Some say that the intensity of this rivalry dates back to 1835, when the states of Ohio and Michigan nearly went to war over a border dispute. It took Andrew Jackson to cool down their contentious governors, and when the territorial dust settled, Ohio got to keep Toledo and Michigan got its Upper Peninsula. Any latent hostility over the affair apparently moved to the football field in 1897, when the Buckeyes played the Wolverines for the first time and were trounced 34–0. Over the years, the outcome of the Ohio State-Michigan game has determined who wins the Big Ten more than 30 times, and after 1946, the already heated competition started to sizzle because both teams could smell the roses at the annual Pac-10 vs. Big Ten bowl game in Pasadena. OSU coach Woody Hayes disliked the Wolverines so much that he would not say the word "Michigan" and always referred to that university as "the school up north." The story is told that while driving in Michigan, Hayes once ran out of gasoline near the Ohio border. Rather than patronize a Michigan filling station, he got out of his car and *pushed* it across the state line. In 1974, when Hayes's favorite tailback Archie Griffin was rushing his way to a Heisman Trophy, a Wolverine player boasted that the only way Griffin would get a hundred yards against Michigan would be over his dead body. Ohio State responded by calling funeral homes. Michigan commanded the series 13–0–2 from 1897 to 1918, but between 1919 and 1987, it was a 33–33–3 stand-off between the teams and their fervent fans, 106,255 of whom set a National Collegiate Athletic Association regular-season attendance record in Ann Arbor on October 23, 1983. Through 1993, Buckeye coach John Cooper's record against Michigan, was 0–5–1, a stinging series of losses so demoralizing for the Buckeyes that Ohio State President Gordon Gee inexplicably proclaimed 1992's 13–13 tie the greatest football win in the university's history.

MIAMI UNIVERSITY VS. UNIVERSITY OF CINCINNATI

The oldest college football rivalry west of the Alleghenies—and the twelfth oldest in the nation—started on December 8, 1888, at the instigation of Miami University's young president Ethelbert Warfield, a debonair and athletic Princeton graduate. Nursing a knee injury from a practice a few days before, Warfield could not play in the Cincinnati game, but other faculty members did join the Miami team, which was coached by a Shakespeare-loving professor. A driving rain fell on the Miami campus, and the game ended in a soggy scoreless tie. The Miami Redskins have squared off against the Cincinnati Bearcats almost every year since then, with Miami leading the series 53–39–6 at the end of the 1993 season. Perhaps their most fateful meeting, however, occurred in 1950, on another miserable day when several inches of snow and a biting cold gripped Cincinnati's Nippert Stadium. The Redskins-Bearcats game was traditionally scheduled for Thanksgiving, but UC coach Sid Gillman had moved it back two days and caught a major Midwest blizzard. Ohio State was looking for a new head coach, and both Gillman and Miami Coach Woody Hayes were prime candidates. Hayes's Redskins romped through the snow to beat Cincinnati 28–0. The win got Hayes a berth in

> *"I want to get into the shoe business. Tonight."*
>
> —Pete Gillen, after almost being upset by Loyola, 1993

Pete
Gillen

the Salad Bowl (the precursor of today's Fiesta Bowl), where his victory over Arizona State landed him at Ohio State and eventually a permanent place in college coaching history. Gillman was, so to speak, temporarily left out in the cold.

UNIVERSITY OF CINCINNATI VS. XAVIER UNIVERSITY

In recent years, there has been very little courtship (and some would say sportsmanship) between these Cincinnati schools, whose annual basketball contest—dubbed the Crosstown Shootout by the local press—has literally created hoopla in the Queen City. The two universities have all the makings for a natural rivalry: UC, the state school and mega-university with 36,000 students and a proud Bearcat basketball tradition that boasts the likes of Oscar Robertson and Jack Twyman vs. Xavier, the private, Jesuit institution with an enrollment of 8,000 and a proud basketball tradition that includes the

Musketeers' against-all-odds championship in the 1958 National Invitational Tournament. In the late 1980s and early 1990s, the arrival and success of coaches Bob Huggins at UC and Pete Gillen at Xavier added an element of personality conflict that fueled the smoldering feud. Huggins turned Cincinnati's faltering program into National Collegiate Athletic Association championship contenders in 1992 and 1993, while Gillen led the Musketeers to seven NCAA tournament appearances in his first eight seasons at Xavier. Yet their place in the national spotlight only seemed to highlight the differences between them: the brash, brusque, bold, and very public personality Huggins vs. the quiet, contemplative, Robert Frost-quoting Gillen. Given Cincinnati's beleaguered sports scene in the early 1990s, the clash between the coaches became a primary Queen City preoccupation. When Huggins refused to shake Gillen's hand after the Musketeers beat the Bearcats in overtime in January, 1994, the incident was the talk of the town, and veteran Cincinnati sportswriter Paul Daugherty declared the UC-Xavier competition to be "the best city rivalry in America."

" There are times during Cincinnati basketball games when the only thing higher than Huggins' blood pressure is his decibel count."

—Paul Daugherty, on Bob Huggins

Bob Huggins

103

Massillon Tigers vs. Canton McKinley Bulldogs

The backyard competition between the neighboring towns of Massillon and Canton is not only Ohio's oldest high school football rivalry, but also arguably the most fabled one in the nation. The *series* began a century ago, in 1894, when Canton beat Massillon 16–6, but their *rivalry* is largely a byproduct of the advent of professional football in northeast Ohio. In 1903, sports reporter Edward Stewart, in Massillon, started Ohio's first pro football team. It was nicknamed the Tigers because Stewart found a good deal on some striped jerseys. A year later, the Bulldogs football club in Canton also went pro, and the two teams tried to outdo each other by attracting top players. When the Tigers met the Bulldogs for a two-game season finale in 1906, the Canton squad included several men from Massillon.

Each team won a game and a playoff was being planned, when the Massillon newspaper charged that the Canton coach had rigged the contest in a gambling scheme. A much-publicized fist fight between outraged fans and the disgraced Bulldogs players escalated into a minor riot in a Canton hotel, and the scandal blackened pro football's tender reputation for years. In 1915, the Bulldogs hired the phenomenal all-around athlete and Olympic champion Jim Thorpe to play for $250 per game. Fans came by the thousands to watch him, and Thorpe's extraordinary talents made the Bulldogs the top dogs in pro football, as they downed the Tigers to claim three unofficial world championships. When the forerunner of the National Football League was formed in Canton in 1920, the Massillon-Canton rivalry was permanently transferred to the town's high school teams. The *prep* Tigers and Bulldogs had a long but erratic history until 1919,

" There have been a few football games before. Yale has faced Princeton. Harvard has tackled Penn, and Michigan and Chicago have met in one or two steamy affairs. But these were not the Real Product when measured by the football standard set by the warring factions of Stark County, Ohio, now posing in the football limelight."

—legendary sports writer Grantland Rice on the old Massillon-Canton rivalry

105

when they started squaring off once every year. Thanks to Canton McKinley, the budding football genius Paul Brown got off to a rocky start as the Massillon High coach in the 1930s. Canton handily tamed his Tigers three years in a row, and some folks in Massillon still claim that the only thing that saved Brown's job—and by extension his brilliant future in football—was that halfback Bob Glass scored a touchdown in 1935 to finally beat the Bulldogs 6–0. The Tigers had a glorious season in 1940, when they racked up 477 points against their opponents and were not only unbeaten but unscored upon until the Canton McKinley game. The Bulldogs scored a solitary touchdown, and those six points spoiled an otherwise perfect year for Massillon. The series came to a 25–25–5 draw in 1950, when Massillon defeated McKinley 33–0. Although Canton lays claim to the longest winning streak—11 games—between 1894 and 1906, Massillon has had more streaks, scored more points, and won more games. At their 99th contest in 1993, the Bulldogs beat the Tigers 21–13, but Massillon still had the lead in the series at 53–41–5. The game between Massillon and Canton McKinley is always the last one of their respective seasons, and it routinely attracts 20,000 devoted, blatantly biased, anything-but-impartial fans. Perhaps because Massillon is a far smaller city and has only one high school, the rivalry is celebrated more intently in Tiger territory, where residents practically paint the town orange and black as old grads migrate back for the parade and traditional bonfire. On November 5, 1994, the old rivals met for the landmark game that determined for the 100th time who got bragging rights in Stark County. As one Massillon resident once observed, "We talk football all winter, especially the McKinley game, and it's a long winter in Ohio, so it's a good idea to be a winner."

PIQUA INDIANS VS. TROY TROJANS

Ohio's oldest continuous high school football rivalry is the Battle of Miami, which has been fought every year since 1899 between the adjacent Great Miami River towns of Troy and Piqua. Apparently, some latent antagonism over an old, hard-fought battle between the two towns concerning where the Miami County Courthouse should be located—it's in Troy, and the statue on the dome was placed with her back toward Piqua—is now played out on their high school football fields. Both the Trojans and the Indians are football titans in Miami County, and their followers routinely swell the teams' respective stadiums to witness their annual contest. It is said that school officials have even threatened to fire coaches if they fail to win. Over the years, the Trojans and Indians have been surprisingly evenly matched, and when they met in regular season play in October, 1992, the series was tied at 50 wins, 50 losses, and 6 ties. The Trojans got the edge with a 22–7 win over the Indians, only to have Piqua settle the score with a 20–7 victory a few weeks later when they met for Ohio's Division I, Region 2 championship. Thus, the series was again deadlocked 51–51–6. Although Troy can claim the longest winning streak with six consecutive games between 1976 and 1981, Piqua has enjoyed winning streaks four times: 1900–1903, 1924–1927, 1934–1938, and 1964–69. From 1969 through 1972, Troy trounced Piqua every year, thanks largely to the services of Gordon Bell, a talented running back who routinely rushed for hundreds of yards and scored touchdowns on the first play of scrimmage.

Gordon Bell later found fame playing for the University of Michigan and the New York Giants, and the Piqua coach reportedly was so relieved to see him graduate from high school that he publicly offered to present Bell with his diploma at Troy's commencement.

Ohio's influence on an Irish stew of men, means, and methods

The University of Notre Dame has the winningest record in college football. Between 1887 and 1992, the Indiana school went 712–210-41, for an unsurpassed .761 winning percentage. The Fighting Irish have had more Heisman Trophy winners—seven— than any other university, and two of their former coaches—Knute Rockne and Frank Leahy—are the most successful in the history of major college teams, having won, respectively, .881 and .864 of the games they coached. Notre Dame is also one of only four universities to have won each of the major post season bowl games: Rose, Orange, Sugar, and Cotton. There is arguably no school in the nation with a stronger gridiron tradition than Notre Dame, where football is indeed the stuff of legends. The university may not be located in Ohio, but Ohioans have not allowed a mere state line to stand in their way. They quite literally have played a major part in the traditions, passions, lore, and legacy that have not only made the Irish a success autumn after autumn but also developed such a national following among fans that many have called Notre Dame America's college football team.

THE CAST OF CHARACTERS:

KNUTE ROCKNE

The self-described "lone Norse Protestant in a stronghold of Irish Catholics," Rockne was the coach who transformed Notre Dame football from a footnote to a front page sport. The combination of his personal charm and spectacular gridiron success not only made Notre Dame synonymous with college football, but also did much raise the public enthusiasm that made football a national spectator sport. At the time of his death in a plane crash in 1931, Rockne was probably the best-known coach in the country, and the years since then have only seemed to enhance his esteem. Rockne was not an innovator, but a brilliant motivator and tireless adapter who deftly borrowed techniques to his teams' best advantage. His seminal adaptation, which was the foundation of his subsequent coaching reputation and achievements, was the use of the forward pass while he was captain of Notre Dame's varsity in 1913. The forward pass had been around for years, but as a technique employing a clumsy egg-shaped football more suitable for kicking than throwing, it was widely disdained by coaches, who preferred to employ brute force. In the summer of 1913, Rockne and Gus Dorais figured out how to make maximum use of the forward pass, and they did it at Ohio's Cedar Point resort on Lake Erie. Since both of them had jobs as lifeguards, quarterback Dorais and end Rockne spent long hours on the beach practicing how to best throw and catch a football. Dorais discovered that by holding the ball by its end and throwing it overhand, he gave the ball a spinning movement that significantly enhanced its speed, accuracy, and distance. When they returned to Notre Dame in the fall, Irish coach Jesse Harper tested their "passing routine" in the season's opening game. Notre Dame demolished Ohio Northern 87–0, but the team—and their forward pass—didn't attract any real attention until the Irish met the Army on November 1. In the surprise upset of the year, the small, obscure school from Indiana mercilessly used the forward pass to beat the eastern football colossus, 35–13. The underdog Irish had arrived at West Point so poorly equipped that the players had to share their shoes during the game, but they departed as conquering football heroes, who had, as the *New York Times* declared, "flashed the most sensational football ever seen in the East." The Irish proved the effectiveness of the forward pass that day, and Notre Dame as well as the game of football would never be the same.

"I don't want anybody going out there to die for dear old Notre Dame. Hell, I want you fighting to stay alive!"

—*Knute Rockne*

BONNIE SKILES ROCKNE

While at Cedar Point during that fateful summer of 1913, Rockne met Bonnie Skiles, a young woman from Kenton who was also working at the resort. On July 15 of the next year, they were married by Rev. William Murphy at Saints Peter and Paul church in Sandusky. Bonnie became the rock upon which Rockne relied, "mothering" him as well as the boys on his teams with home-cooked meals. She claimed that she could always tell when her husband had invited players to their house because Rockne and his boys always rearranged the furniture into play formations. Since Bonnie was a devout Catholic, Rockne eventually yielded to her—not to mention the campus—influence and converted after his mother, a staunch Lutheran, died. The story is told that he officially became a Catholic in 1925, on the morning of the game against Northwestern. By halftime, the Wildcats were leading the Irish 10–0, and in the locker room, Rockne reportedly said to his players, "This is a hell of a religion you got me into. On my first day in it, you let yourself be pushed around by a Methodist school." The Irish, of course, came back fighting and won 13–10.

RAY "IRON EICH" EICHENLAUB

A 225-pound fullback from Columbus, Eichenlaub was a teammate of Knute Rockne and Gus Dorais, and he earned his nickname because of his bone-jarring way of plowing through opposing linemen. In the historic 1913 game against Army, he was the infantry that complemented the surprise air attack Dorais waged with the forward pass. Eichenlaub was the biggest man on the Notre Dame team, and he sealed the school's victory by scoring the Irish's last two touchdowns. Eichenlaub was inducted into the College Football Hall of Fame in 1972.

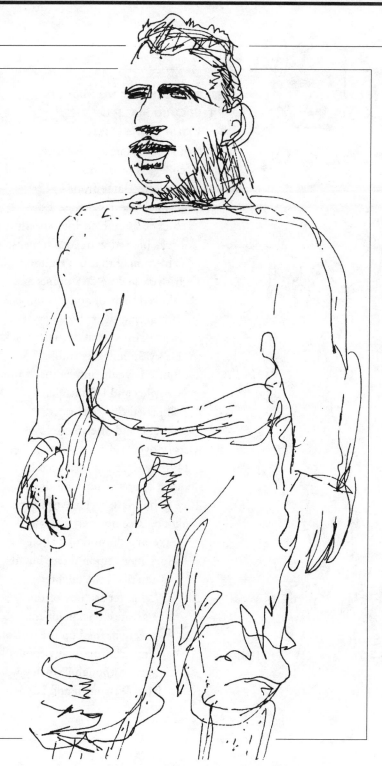

Iron Eich graduated from Columbus East High in 1910 and became its first All-American. He was headed for Princeton until a Notre Dame coach invited Eich to lunch. Four sandwiches later, he was on his way to South Bend.

—*Jay Eichenlaub*

Ray Eichenlaub

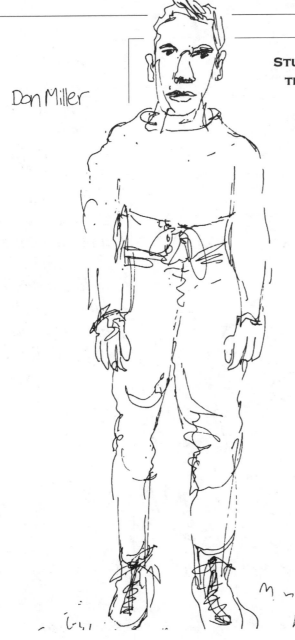

Don Miller

STUHLDREHER AND MILLER: THE OHIO HALF OF THE FOUR HORSEMEN

The most famous backfield in college football history belonged to Notre Dame from 1922 through the 1925 Rose Bowl. Rockne assembled four speedy backs blessed with such impeccable timing that the Fighting Irish racked up 755 points and allowed their opponents only 108 during their three very lucky Irish seasons. Quarterback Harry Stuhldreher, fullback Elmer Layden, and halfback Jim Crowley and Don Miller comprised this celebrated backfield, and after their 1924 victory over Army on October 18, 1924, they were immortalized by the eloquent sportswriter Grantland Rice in his New York newspaper column. Rice not only bestowed the literary allusion of "The Four Horsemen" upon them, but also described the talented quartet as "one of the greatest backfields that ever churned up the turf of any gridiron in any football age." Although Crowley was from Wisconsin and Layden was from Iowa, Stuhldreher and Miller were both native Ohioans. Miller was born in Defiance on March 29, 1902, while Stuhldreher was born in Massillon, October 14, 1901. The Four Horsemen's last game together was the 1925 Rose Bowl, in which they bested Pop Warner's Stanford team, 27–10. All of the horsemen played professional football for a short time, and all were inducted into the National Football Foundation Hall of Fame. Stuhldreher, an All-American, later became the head football coach at Villanova. Miller, a future president of the United States Attorneys Association, became the U.S. District Attorney for the Northern District of Ohio.

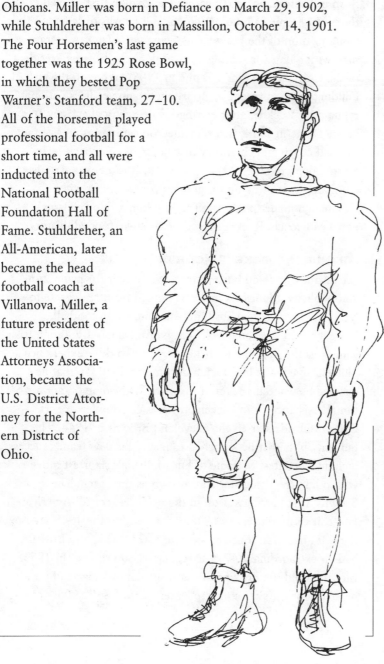

Harry Stuhldreher

"Outlined against a blue-gray October sky, The Four Horsemen rode again. In dramatic lore, they are known as famine, pestilence, destruction, and death. Their real names are Stuhldreher, Miller, Crowley, and Layden..."

—Grantland Rice, immortalizing the Four Horsemen

FATHER JOHN W. CAVANAUGH

Born in Leetonia in 1870, Father Cavanaugh first arrived on the Notre Dame campus at age 16, and he was ordained in the Congregation of the Holy Cross seven years later. A literate man with a flair for writing and speaking, he became President of the University of Notre Dame in 1905, taking on the task of building its endowment by polishing the university's national reputation. Rockne, after getting his degree in chemistry at Notre Dame in 1914, had remained on campus as an assistant football coach and chemistry instructor. When coach Jesse Harper departed Notre Dame in 1918, Rockne was seriously considering also leaving for greener pastures. But when Cavanaugh made the decision to hire him as Notre Dame's new head coach, Rockne stayed on to make football history.

ARTHUR B. "MICKEY" McBRIDE

A colorful Cleveland businessman with a flair for promotion and publicity, McBride's interests ranged from real estate to radio stations. He had absolutely no interest in football, however, until his son enrolled at Notre Dame. A Fighting Irish game was the first one McBride ever saw, and his experience at Notre Dame made him such a devoted football fan that he decided he wanted a team of his own. With some organizational assistance from Cleveland Rams co-founder Robert Gries, McBride started the Cleveland Browns in 1944. The publicity blitz that he launched to insure his new team's success included a contest to name it, but McBride's smartest move was to hire the rising star Paul Brown as the coach. The Browns' first playing season in the now-defunct All-American Football Conference was 1946. By the end of the 1949 season, the team had won four consecutive AAFC titles, and Brown had an extraordinary 47–4–3 regular season record. In 1953, McBride sold the Browns to a consortium of Cleveland businessmen for the then-unprecedented sum of $600,000.

Edgar "Rip" Miller

The Four Horsemen could never have known success—let alone fame—without the support of the deft Notre Dame linemen collectively known as "The Seven Mules." One of the mules who helped the horsemen trample their football foes was Rip Miller, a jug-eared tackle from Canton, Ohio. In high school, he had taped his protruding ears to his head to keep them from being "ripped" off by opposing players. Despite the rivalry of their respective high schools back in Canton and Massillon, Miller and Stuhldreher became fast friends and teammates at Notre Dame. Although the 1925 Rose Bowl marked the last college appearance of the Horsemen and Mules, Miller remained on the gridiron as a coach, eventually taking the helm at Navy. He was inducted into the National Football Foundation Hall of Fame in 1966.

Ralph Guglielmi

A standout athlete at Grandview Heights High near Columbus, Guglielmi almost went to Ohio State in 1951, but changed his mind at the last minute and went to Notre Dame where his arm made him one of the most celebrated Irish quarterbacks. Guglielmi combined exceptional all-around ability—he was described as "a better passer than Angelo Bertelli, a better field general than Johnny Lujack, and more daring than Bob Williams"—with superb passing and running skills. In his senior year of 1954, Guglielmi was named an All-American and won the Walter Camp Trophy as the best back in the nation.

Alan Page

With ten players named All-Americans, Notre Dame's 1966 team was arguably the best that Ara Parseghian ever coached. One of the favored Irish that year was defensive end Alan Page, who parlayed his Irish exploits into a pro football career with the Minnesota Vikings and Chicago Bears. A former football

Notre Dame National Champion teams coached by Ohioans (which also happened to have perfect— no losses, no ties—regular season records as well):

Ara Parseghian, 1973

Lou Holtz, 1988

star at Canton Central Catholic, Page was a first round draft choice of the Vikings in 1967, and in 1972, he became the first defensive player selected the National Football League's Most Valuable Player. Relying on his speed and savvy to disrupt plays, Page was selected for the Pro Bowl every year from 1968 to 1976, and he played with the Vikings in four Super Bowl games. Page was inducted into the Pro Football Hall of Fame in 1988, the first Canton native ever selected for his hometown's most hallowed hall. In 1978, Page was graduated from the University of Minnesota law school, and he is now a justice on the Minnesota Supreme Court.

ARA PARSEGHIAN

Born in Akron in 1923, Parseghian was an All-Ohio halfback at Miami University in the late 1940s, and he played a year for the Cleveland Browns before a hip injury ended his pro career. Parseghian went back to Miami, where he was an assistant coach under Woody Hayes, only to become, at age 26, the Redskins' head coach when Hayes went to Ohio State. After five successful seasons at Miami, he moved on to head coaching positions at Northwestern and then Notre Dame. An almost-charismatic coach who demanded much of himself and his players, Parseghian led the Irish to 11 winning season between 1964 and 1975, including five bowl games and two national championships in 1966 and 1973. His record at Notre Dame was a stellar 95–17–4.

GERRY FAUST

Faust was raised on football in Dayton, where his father, Gerry, Sr., was the coach at Chaminade High School. A quarterback at the University of Dayton in the late 1950s, Faust's first coaching job was as an assistant to his father. But when Faust, Jr. went to Cincinnati's Moeller High School in 1963, he carved a name for himself in the record books as one of the nation's best high school coaches. In his 18 unsurpassed seasons at the Cincinnati school, Faust compiled a 174–17–2 record, yielding five state championships for the school and an astronomical .907 winning percentage for himself. When Notre Dame tapped him for its head coach in 1981, hopes were high that Faust could work his prep magic on the college level. Unfortunately, it might have been easier for Faust to deal with the devil than with the demands of the Irish fans. Known as the quintessential "nice guy," Faust finished his five-year contract at Notre Dame with a 30–26–1 record, a showing that would be considered decent at many schools, but was a disaster given the traditionally winning ways of the Irish. Faust is now head coach at the University of Akron.

LOU HOLTZ

The son of a bus driver and a nurse, Holtz was raised in East Liverpool and is a graduate of Kent State University. In 1985, he took over the Notre Dame football program where his fellow Ohioan Faust left off, rebuilding the team into the national power that the ND faithful have come to know, love, and *expect*. Holtz had previously coached at William and Mary, North Carolina State, Arkansas, and Minnesota, taking the Razorbacks to the Orange, Fiesta, Sugar, and Gator Bowls. A no-nonsense disciplinarian known for his motivational skills, Holtz is already a legend-in-the-making at Notre Dame, where he finished the 1993 regular season with a 76–19–1 record, for a .797 winning percentage. In his eight seasons at Notre Dame, Holtz has taken the Irish to one national championship (1988), and seven major bowl games, including the victory over Texas A&M in the 1994 Cotton Bowl.

HARRY "THE BLOND BEAST" BAUJAN

Between 1913 and 1916, he played end on Knute Rockne's first five history-making teams. Baujan then served in World

While he was growing up in Cleveland, Les Horvath's dream was to play for the Irish, but Notre Dame considered him too small. Horvath measured up, however, at Ohio State, where he won a Heisman Trophy. Cincinnati's Roger Staubach also wanted to go Notre Dame, but the university declined to give him a scholarship. Instead, he went to the Naval Academy and got a Heisman Trophy.

War I and had a brief pro career with the Massillon Tigers before becoming head football coach at the University of Dayton in 1923. It was Rockne who had recommended Baujan for the Flyers job, and two years later, Rockne came to Dayton for the dedication of the football stadium that would eventually be renamed in his protege's honor. Although Baujan earned his beastly nickname because of the old-fashioned discipline that he strictly imposed on his players, he nonetheless launched the "modern era" of UD football, transforming the flat Flyers into one of the strongest small college teams in Ohio. Never outscored in a season, Baujan retired from coaching with a 124–64–8 record after the 1946 season, then served as Dayton's athletic director until 1964. He was inducted into the College Football Hall of Fame in 1990.

LANDMARKS:

NOTRE DAME STADIUM

It is known as the "House that Rockne Built" because the coach not only made Notre Dame football a "first rate production" but also lobbied for a first rate sports facility to accommodate the growing horde of Irish fans. The stadium was built by the Osborn Engineering Company of Cleveland in 1930. At that time, the Osborn company was renowned as "the stadium builder of the nation," for the firm had designed such premier facilities as Yankee Stadium in New York, Comiskey Park in Chicago, Fenway Park in Boston, and university stadiums at Purdue, Indiana, Minnesota, Northwestern, and Michigan. Although Notre Dame's stadium is a smaller version of the one the company built at the University of Michigan in 1927, Rockne had a definite hand in its design. He insisted, for example, that the stadium be strictly a football facility and that the area between the playing field and stands be made as small as possible. Notre Dame Stadium was also the nation's first college stadium financed by pre-leasing the boxes and best seats, a financial strategy that succeeded even in a Depression economy because of the phenomenal number of Irish faithful. The stadium, of course, did not disappoint the fans, for it became one of the true landmarks of American sports, an incomparable place of legends where Heisman winners and All-American winners romped into history. In turn, at least three generations of the faithful have made Saturday afternoon pilgrimages to Notre Dame stadium, which except for an ill-scheduled game on Thanksgiving Day, 1973, has been sold out for every home game since 1967.

THE 1935 OHIO STATE–NOTRE DAME GAME

Many consider it to be the game of the century. If not, the 1935 showdown between the Irish and the Buckeyes certainly ranks as one of the most talked and written about games in college football history. Both teams were unbeaten and vying for a national championship when they met in Columbus on November 2. Elmer Layden, a former Four Horseman, was now Notre Dame's coach, while the innovative Francis Schmidt was only in his second season as the OSU coach. Even in the throes of the Depression, tickets were selling for $100 each, and 81,000 fans plus some of the nation's premier reporters— Grantland Rice, Damon Runyon, Red Barber—were on hand to watch the battle. By the end of the third quarter, Notre Dame was losing 13–0, and victory seemed certain for the Buckeyes. But in the final thrilling 15 minutes of play, the Irish pulled off three touchdowns—the winning one executed with only half a minute on the clock—to win the game, 18–13. Ronald Reagan, who on that same Saturday was doing play-by-play of the Iowa–Indiana game, kept announcing the OSU-Notre score during his radio broadcast. But when the future President got the 18–13 score, he assumed it was a mistake. Reagan never announced that final score because he thought such a come-from-behind victory was impossible.

The first football game ever played at Cleveland Stadium was between Notre Dame and Navy. The Irish won 12–0 on November 19, 1932. Over the years, they met many times in Cleveland, including the 1945 game when the Irish battled to a 6–6 tie in one of the toughest contests ever waged by either team. Injuries included a concussion, a separated shoulder, and eleven teeth forfeited by the Notre Dame fullback.

119

IRISH COUNTRY:

CEDAR POINT

Knute Rockne not only perfected the forward pass and met his wife at the resort, it also became a part of his personal and professional life. The beach was perhaps his favorite family vacation spot, and he quite rightly regarded it as the place that had marked the turning point of his career. As Notre Dame's coach, he even sent his players to Cedar Point, getting jobs for them as lifeguards so they could repeat the pass practice—and thus the success—he and Dorais had found on the Lake Erie shore.

MASSILLON

Formed just after the turn of the century, the Massillon Tigers were Ohio's first professional football team. The Tigers quickly developed a fierce rivalry with the neighboring Canton Bulldogs, and both teams recruited "name" players from around the country to boost attendance at their games. Notre Dame stars Knute Rockne and Gus Dorias frequently played for Massillon, and among the admiring youngsters who turned out to watch their performance on the gridiron was Harry Stuhldreher, the local boy who in a few years would become one of Coach Rockne's fabled Four Horse-

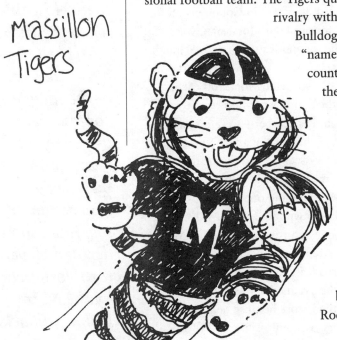

Massillon Tigers

men. Rockne and Dorais were playing for the Tigers in the 1915 game during which Olympic champion Jim Thorpe made his debut as a Canton Bulldog. Early in the first quarter, Rockne tackled Thorpe twice, and the Bulldogs lost yards on both plays. The enormously popular Thorpe reportedly told Rockne, "You shouldn't do that. Look at all those people who paid to see Jim run." And run Thorpe did. On the very next play, he thundered past Rockne and went 60 people-pleasing yards for a touchdown.

DEFIANCE

From this small northwest Ohio town, the sons of Martin and Anne Miller went to Notre Dame, where they became a veritable football dynasty in the early 1900s. Don of the fabled Four Horsemen was the most renowned, but he was only one of several Miller brothers who played for the Irish. Walter Miller, a fullback, was a teammate of George Gipp on Rockne's undefeated 1919 and 1920 teams. Gerry Miller suffered an injury early in his ND career, but still served as a substitute back for his brother Don. While Ray Miller forfeited his starting position on Notre Dame's 1912 team to Rockne and the forward pass, he compensated for his loss after graduation, when he started a law practice in Cleveland and became the mayor of that city in 1932. Halfback Harry "Red" Miller was captain of the 1908 team and the father of two future ND varsity players, Tom and Creighton. Creighton, the spectacular All-American halfback who in 1943 led Notre Dame to its first victory over Michigan since 1909, also became a highly successful attorney in Cleveland, where he joined his uncle Ray in helping to organize the Cleveland Browns.

Notre Dame's nickname no doubt originated with the large number of Irish-Catholic students and faculty members the school once had. But "Fighting Irish" wasn't universally used until the 1920s, when Francis 'Frank' Wallace, a Notre Dame grad from Bellaire, popularized the nickname by writing it in his New York Daily News sports column.

1. OHIO CUP—this annual exhibition game between the Cincinnati Reds and Cleveland Indians is played in Columbus, a middle ground for fans of both teams. Hosted by the minor league Columbus Clippers, the game is traditionally played shortly before the regular season's opening day.

2. ACME–ZIP GAME—one of the best known college football promotions in the country, it began in 1954, when the University of Akron teamed up with Acme food stores to boost attendance at games. Now an annual autumn rite in Akron that attracts some 30,000 people, the event has expanded to include not only a football game and eye-popping half time activities, but also sideshows such as soccer, rugby, and fireworks.

3. GOLD PANTS—every time that Ohio State beats Michigan in football, each of the victorious Buckeye players is presented with a shiny, pair-of-pants-shaped pin. The custom started with a 1934 pep talk by OSU coach Francis Schmidt, who wanted to point out to his players that the worrisome Wolverines put their pants on one leg at a time, just like every other mortal.

4. SCRIPT OHIO—certainly one of college football's most recognized halftime formations, it has been an Ohio State habit since October 24, 1936, when Ohio State band director Eugene Weigel had his 120 musicians march to the French tune *Le Regiment* while they spelled out O-h-i-o in cursive. The size of the OSU band has grown considerably since then, but not nearly so much as the popularity of Script Ohio. Fans seem to regard the formation as being nearly as essential to Buckeye football as the kick off, and a highlight at every halftime is the chosen senior sousaphone player who marches out to dot the "i" in Ohio. Weigel, by the way, was also responsible for making Ohio State's marchers an all-brass band. He benched all the woodwinds in 1934, explaining that only brass instruments could do justice to the acoustics of a stadium.

5. HANG ON SLOOPY—the Ohio State band made this song the Buckeyes' unofficial touchdown anthem, playing it whenever the they mounted a scoring drive during their 1970s football heyday. Originally recorded by the McCoys, a Dayton band, *Sloopy* later became Ohio's official Rock Song.

6. THE MARCHING 110—the Ohio University band, which bills itself as "The Most Exciting Band in the Land" and serves that *other* state school in Athens. It is renowned for performing creative, high-energy halftime shows at Bobcat football games.

7. A Y ZIGGY ZOOMBA—the unofficial fight song of Bowling Green State University, it is always sung by the football team following a win. Of unknown origin, it was thrust upon the nation's eardrums by Mike Weger, a former BGSU All-American and Detroit Lion halfback who sang it in the movie *Paper Lion*.

8. VICTORY BELL—originally located in Old Main on the Miami University campus, the bell serves as a trophy for the venerable Miami-Cincinnati football rivalry. To the victor of the annual game belongs the bell, which is painted on one side with Miami's colors (red and white) and on the other side with Cincinnati's (red and black). Ohio State also has a Victory Bell, presented as a gift by the Class of 1943. It hangs in the southeast tower of Ohio Stadium and is sounded every time an OSU team wins a game.

9. THE PUMPKIN SMASH—Before their annual bout with the Bowling Green State University Falcons, the Miami University football team orders a slew of pumpkins. Then after the game, the Redskins get together and smash the pumpkins . . . but only if they're the victors. No one is certain how this custom began. It may have something to do with the Falcons' colors being burnt orange and seal brown, a combination that supposedly was chosen because a Bowling Green faculty

" *Ay Ziggy*
Zoomba
Zoomba
Zoomba
Ay Ziggy
Zoomba
Zoomba Ze
Ay Ziggy
Zoomba
Zoomba
Zoomba
Ay Ziggy
Zoomba
Zoomba Zi

Roll 'em down
you BG warriors
Roll 'em down
and win for
BGSU."

—Bowling Green fight song

"Something seized me."

—*New York pharmacist, explaining why he was wearing a Chief Wahoo cap*

member noticed the eye-catching colors on a hat worn by a woman he saw on a bus trip to Toledo.

10. THE PEACE PIPE—this trophy travels each year to the winner of the Bowling Green-University of Toledo football game. The tradition originally started in the late 1940s with a six-foot wooden pipe that was passed back and forth between the schools' respective basketball teams.

11. THE WAGON WHEEL—in 1870, when John Buchtel, a prosperous farm equipment manufacturer from Akron, was searching for a place to start a college, he drove his wagon to Kent to look at some land. When his wagon got hopelessly bogged down in the mud and his horses ran away, Buchtel decided to locate the college in Akron. Kent State University was eventually built on the site Buchtel rejected, and Buchtel College became the University of Akron. Years later, one of the wagon wheels that had been buried in the mud during Buchtel's fateful trip was accidentally uncovered, and Kent State's Dean of Men suggested it would make a fine trophy for the winner of the Akron-Kent football game. The wheel was painted blue and gold to match the colors of both universities, and it has been passed back and forth between their victorious teams ever since.

♦ **12. CHIEF WAHOO**—the grinning Indian brave logo used by the Cleveland Indians was created by *Cleveland Plain Dealer* cartoonist Fred Reinert and first appeared on players' jerseys in

Chief Wahoo

1947. For years, his huge image mounted high atop Cleveland Stadium smiled over the city.

13. THE STEEL-TIRE TROPHY—awarded since 1976 to the winner of the Youngstown State-University of Akron football game, the trophy symbolizes not only the rivalry between the schools, but also the industries that once put their respective cities on the map.

14. HAGAR AND HELGA—based on the cartoon characters created by Dik Browne, this costumed duo appears as mascots to the Cleveland State Vikings.

15. ZIPPY—the University of Akron selected a kangaroo for its mascot in 1953. Proponents of this most unusual choice pointed out that the animal "is fast, agile, and powerful—all the necessary qualities of an athlete." Zippy made his debut when an Akron student crawled inside a kangaroo costume at the 1954 football game with Wittenberg, which also happened to be the university's first Acme-Zip game.

16. CARRY BACK—the Ohio colt that won both the Kentucky Derby and the Preakness, but lost the Triple Crown at the Belmont Stakes in 1961. The three-year old was that year's top money winner and was later elected to the National Museum of Racing Hall of Fame.

17. SCHOTTZIE—the most famous St. Bernard in Ohio belongs to Cincinnati Reds owner Marge Schott, who has made her much-loved pet into the team's unofficial mascot. Actually, there have been two Schottzies. The first Schottzie, who appeared on national television with David Letterman, died in 1991. Several months later, Mrs. Schott acquired a successor St. Bernard and christened her Schottzie 02. Schottzie 02 quickly made a name for herself at Riverfront Stadium, where she roamed the AstroTurf before games and left surprises for the Reds players.

♦ The regal schnozz of stellar shortstop Roger Peckinpaugh of Cleveland, who was the AL's MVP in 1925 with Washington and later managed the Indians, is said to have been the inspiration for the Chief Wahoo logo.

18. OBIE—the *real* tiger cub that is the high school mascot in football-focused Massillon. Obie gets his name from the first letters of the school colors—orange and black—and is the only live wild animal high school mascot in the state.

19. OLD ABE AND VICTOR—pressed into service as mascots during varsity games at Ashland College, they are the most well-known of the many live eagles that inexplicably began roosting on the campus after the school changed its nickname from Purple Titans to Eagles.

20. SIR WINSALOT AND PAWS—these noble beasts are the live bobcats that have been used as mascots at Ohio University football games.

21. MAUDINE ORMSBY—in 1926, a Miss Ormsby was nominated for Ohio State's Homecoming Queen. Miss Ormsby turned out to be a Holstein cow sponsored by the College of Agriculture. Thanks to some suspiciously stuffed ballot boxes, she got the most votes, and since the election committee couldn't determine which Homecoming Queen ballots were legitimate, Maudine was made the winner. She got to ride in the homecoming parade, but was barred from the dance.

22. OORANG INDIANS—In 1922, Walter Lingo, who owned the Oorang Kennels in the Marion County burg of LaRue organized a professional football team to publicize his airedales. He wanted the team to consist of players who were all or part Indian, and recruited the legendary Jim Thorpe to organize the team. Thorpe was a gifted athlete and the only person in history to win both the pentathalon and decathalon in the same Olympics. Thorpe's Olympic glory, however, was soon tarnished. The next year, he was stripped of his medals for being paid to play baseball in 1909. Thorpe then played professional baseball for a few years before switching to football and joining the Canton Bulldogs. When the forerunner of the National Football League was organized in Canton, he also served briefly as its figurehead president, lending his prestige to the fledgling organization. Lingo's Oorang Indians were a traveling team, and as expected, Thorpe attracted crowds. Halftime entertainment included dog shows and exhibitions of Indian singing, dancing, and rituals. Although the roster included future Pro Football Hall of Famers Thorpe and Joe Guyon, the Oorang Indians had two losing seasons and disbanded in 1923.

23. ALL-STAR ACCIDENTS—

Ohio baseball players have twice been involved in All-Star Game mishaps that had unhappy endings for other major leaguers. In the 1937 All-Star Game, Cleveland Indian Earl Averill indirectly caused the end of St. Louis pitcher Dizzy Dean's fabled career. Averill hit a line drive off Dean that

"Jim never used his arms in orthodox tackling style. Instead, he hunched his shoulders and rammed his 210 pounds into the ball carrier. Jim racked up an awful lot of ball carriers that way, particularly when he happened to be wearing his 'special' shoulder pads, which were reinforced with a stiffening layer of sheet metal."

—George Halas, on playing against Jim Thorpe

127

hit the pitcher in the foot. Dean didn't allow the fracture to properly heal, and the negative affect of the injury soon ended his playing days. In 1970, the All-Star classic was held at Riverfront Stadium in Cincinnati. With two out in the bottom of the 12th, Pete Rose of the Cincinnati Reds singled and dashed for home, where he crashed into Cleveland catcher Ray Fosse. The collision caused Fosse to drop the ball, giving Rose the winning run for the National League. Rose's hit was so hard that it dislocated Fosse's shoulder. Rose was roundly vilified, but he took the insults far better than Fosse did the injury. The catcher never fully recovered, and Rose's impact on Fosse was to shorten his major league career.

24. WATERLOO WONDERS—a fabled high school basketball team from the tiny Lawrence County village of Waterloo, the Wonders had a 56-game winning streak and won consecutive state championships in 1934 and 1935, while becoming Ohio's all-time high school basketball legend. Waterloo's playing style was unorthodox and showy; they might bounce the ball off the floor into the basket, or two players might go to the bench and eat popcorn while their teammates played three-on-five. They knew ball-handling, back-hand passing, and run-and-gun. They developed the pivot, highly uncommon then in prep play. They beat Mark Center 40–26 for the state title, and Orlyn Roberts, in the three games, had scored 69 points, still a record. After their first Class B championship, they began to play A schools. They didn't lose for 56 games. They barnstormed around Ohio in their young coach's black Chevrolet sedan and, according to writer Danny Fulks, "they were, in unique combination, consummate basketball players and deliberate clowns. They mastered the range of conventional court tactics and then moved beyond them to innovations that extended the limits of the game." In mid-winter, they were scheduled to play at Painesville, east of Cleveland, but the team ran into a snowstorm north of Columbus and called Painesville to say they might not make it. When the announcement was made in the packed Painesville gym, no one left. When The Wonders arrived at 1 a.m., the gym was still full. During the early part of February, 1935, they beat five Class A schools in six days and, the next week, beat the tallest team in Kentucky, the famous Piner Giants from Kenton County, who averaged 6' 5". Unheard-of crowds swelled primitive gyms, and the boys became celebrities, earning the program enough from 10 and 20-cent tickets to allow them to stay in hotels where they learned how to tip the bellboys and order off menus. They lost only three games in 1935, on their way to their second state title. Author Dick Burdette pointed out that other teams have had more impressive scoring records, and may have had better defenses but none had more overall skill, showmanship, and staying power. "The odds were infinity-to-one," he wrote, "but the Waterloo Wonders became the most colorful, beloved high school combination in Ohio basketball history."

The kids learned how to play in a hayloft where Orlyn Roberts, his cousin Wyman Roberts, and Stewart Wiseman practiced with a handful of rags masquerading as a ball, tossed through an old iron ring off a wagon. In the hayloft, the boys imagined the size of the trophy for winning the state championship. It would have to be, they concluded, "surely as large as a kitchen stove."

129

> *"This isn't a ball-park; it's a cow pasture. A guy ought to have a horse to play the outfield."*
>
> —*Babe Ruth on Cleveland Stadium, 1933*

♦**25. CLEVELAND MUNICIPAL STADIUM**—the nation's first municipally funded football stadium, this landmark along Lake Erie was completed in 1931 and was designed to seat more than 71,000 people. The behemoth cost $3.5 million and was supposedly built to entice the 1932 Olympics to Cleveland.

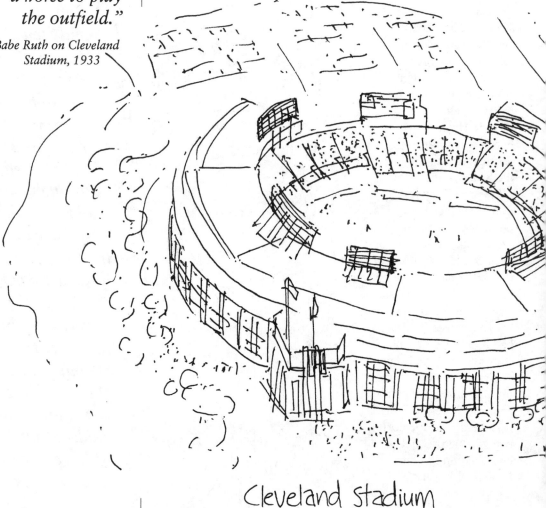

Cleveland stadium

If so, the bait didn't work, for the summer games went to Los Angeles that year. Nonetheless, Cleveland taxpayers have gotten their money's worth over the years. Along with the Indians and Browns who serve as the hometown good sports, the stadium has hosted the 1931 Max Schmeling–Young Stribling heavyweight championship bout, the Beatles, and the Metropolitan Opera. Joe DiMaggio's unparalleled 56-game hitting streak ended at Cleveland Stadium in 1941, and Frank Robinson hit a home run there in his first at-bat as a player/ manager on April 8, 1975. The stadium was even the backdrop for *The Babe Ruth Story*, a made-for-TV movie filmed there in 1991. Through 1993, Cleveland Stadium was the largest facility in the U.S. used by both a major league baseball team and a National Football League team. The Indians departed at the end of the 1993 season for their new field of dreams, the ultra modern Gateway sports complex in downtown Cleveland.

26. BEER NIGHT RIOT—on the night of June 4, 1974, the Indians offered beer for ten cents a cup in an effort to draw fans to Cleveland Stadium for their game against the Texas Rangers. In the bottom of the ninth inning, the score was tied, and the Indians had two outs with men on first and third. Suddenly a fan ran out and tried to separate Texas right fielder Jeff Burroughs from his glove. When Burroughs resisted, more fans swarmed out of the stands, and soon a crowd estimated at several thousand people was rioting on the field. Efforts to restore order were useless, and umpire Nestor Chylak declared the game forfeited to the Rangers.

♦*When the Indians moved to Cleveland Stadium in 1932, pitcher Mel Harder initiated the mound in their inaugural game on July 31. Harder, alas, lost the game to the Phillies 1–0. Fittingly, when the Indians vacated the stadium in October, 1993, they brought back the 84-year-old Harder to throw out the final pitch in the closing ceremonies.*

131

27. ICKEY SHUFFLE—the celebrated end zone victory dance performed in the late 1980s by Cincinnati Bengals star running back Ickey Woods. Described by one sportswriter as "a hip, a hop, a skip, and a spike," Ickey performed his shuffle whenever he scored a touchdown. When the Bengals appeared in the 1989 Super Bowl, the shuffle was analyzed by a scholar at the American Academy of Religion, who declared the National Football League championship game to be American culture's major religious festival and Ickey's dance the high point of the day's sacred rituals.

28. DAWG POUND—the bleacher seats located at the open end of Cleveland Stadium, where Browns fans are known for antics that range from putting on mutt-like masks to throwing eggs and dog biscuits at players on rival teams. The dawgs' rowdiness is so well-known in the NFL that when Cincinnati fans threw snowballs a few years back, Bengals coach Sam Wyche chastised the crowd by saying, "You don't live in Cleveland."

29. ADA, OHIO—the Wilson Sporting Goods Co. in this Hardin County town produces thousands of footballs each year, including the regulation ones used by National Football League teams.

30. OHIO STADIUM—the Columbus stadium where Ohio State pursues the glories of the gridiron every autumn is one of college football's classic landmarks. It was dubbed "The House That Chic Built" because Chic Harley's thrilling long distance touchdown runs brought so many fans into the stands that the university had to have a bigger, better place to put them. Designed to accommodate 66,210 people, many people doubted that Ohio Stadium would ever be filled when it opened on October 7, 1922. Two weeks later, 71,000 fans showed up for the dedication game against Michigan. The stadium has been expanded several times and now holds 91,470, making it the nation's fourth largest college football facility.

31. ALL-AMERICAN SOAP BOX DERBY—the Soap Box Derby is an American original that became an American institution soon after the first race was held on a steep Dayton hill in 1933. Myron Scott, a Dayton newspaper photographer, saw some boys coasting down a hill in homemade cars and decided to turn their amusement into an organized event and present the winner with a trophy. It was so successful—some 40,000 people showed up to watch 330 boys race down Dayton's Burkhardt Hill—that the Chevrolet automobile company became the derby's sponsor and turned it into a national race. Chevrolet moved the Derby to Akron in 1935, and the nation's one and only "Gravity Grand Prix" has been held there ever since.

32. TOURNAMENT OF CHAMPIONS—the most prestigious event in men's bowling, the Tournament of Champions is considered the "crown jewel" of Professional Bowlers Association tournaments. The event has been held at Riviera Lanes in Fairlawn since it began in 1965 and is sponsored by rubber companies in the Akron area.

33. LITTLE BROWN JUG—the Jug is the most illustrious event in the world of harness racing. Along with the Cane Pace at Yonkers Raceway and the Messenger Stake at Roosevelt Raceway, it comprises the Triple Crown for three-year old pacers. Named for a famous horse that once raced on dirt roads, the internationally known Jug is the only major harness event still held at a county fairgrounds, and every September, it annually attracts some 50,000 people to Delaware. The race's official song is, of course, *Little Brown Jug*, and the trophy is a plain, but prized brown jug with a bronze plaque.

34. CASEY STENGEL—the colorful coach who built the 1950s baseball powerhouse that was the New York Yankees honed the skills he applied to Mantle and Berra as a player/manager with the Toledo in the late 1920s. When he took the Mud Hens to an American Association pennant, the win touched off a celebration in Toledo that lasted three days.

> *"I can remember Jim Hegan reaching over and grabbing a towel to wipe off the plate. I told him there weren't no need of doing anything like that. I gave him this gum wrapper and told him to lay it the long way of home plate. After I split that wrapper a few times with my fast ball, they sort of decided I still had my control."*
>
> *—Satchel Paige on his major league premiere at age 42*

35. SATCHEL PAIGE—Leroy Paige (he was nicknamed Satchel because he worked as a porter at his hometown's railroad station in Alabama) was a stellar performer with black teams, most notably the top notch Pittsburgh Crawfords, in the 1930s. In 1933, he won 21 games in a row, and the next year, he reportedly won 104 of his 105 games. Unfortunately for him—and baseball—his very best days were behind him, and he was well into middle age when the major leagues' color barrier finally crumbled and owner Bill Veeck recruited him for the 1948 Indians. Satchel Paige made his first appearance as a major leaguer on July 9, when he pitched the Cleveland Indians to a 5–3 victory over Washington. In the Indians' 1948 pennant race with New

Satchel Paige

York, Paige proved why he was known as "The Ageless Wonder." Things looked very sweet in the ninth inning for the Yankees, who had no outs and Phil Rizzuto anxiously poised at third. The Indians called for Paige, who on his way to the mound informed Rizzuto, "You ain't goin' nowhere." Paige then summarily struck out the Yankees' next three batters in only ten pitches.

36. BLIZZARD BOWL—the 1950 game Ohio State-Michigan game, which was played in a one of the worst snowstorms ever to hit Ohio. Several inches of snow covered the Ohio Stadium gridiron, the temperature dipped into the single digits, and winds exceeded 25 mph when the Wolverines attacked the Buckeyes on November 25. Field conditions were so bad that Ohio State's total rushing was only 16 yards, and Michigan's was a mere 27. In the stands, more than 50,000 fans toughed out the storm and Ohio State's 9–3 loss. While the "Blizzard Bowl" significantly swelled the fanatic reputation of the Buckeye faithful, it also buried Buckeye coach Wes Fesler, who was frozen out of Ohio State after losing the game.

37. EDDIE ELIAS—an Akron attorney, Elias founded the Professional Bowlers' Association (PBA) in 1958. Although the PBA is now regarded as bowling's equivalent of the major leagues, its first tour consisted of only three cities—Albany, New York; Paramus, New Jersey; and Dayton, Ohio—and the prize money was just $50,000. When Elias pioneered having PBA tournaments televised, he boosted bowling's popularity and the success of his association. The PBA tour now has more than 30 tournaments and awards millions of dollars every year. The association headquarters is still in Akron.

38. JIM JEFFRIES—born in Carrollton in 1875, Jeffries began boxing professionally in his early twenties. He was one of the earliest fighters to use the defensive crouch, which complemented his considerable strength so well that he held the world heavyweight championship from 1899–1905. Jeffries retired undefeated and his winning record would have

> *"Quarter-milers' faces, after what they have asked of themselves, make a driver's license picture look like an oil painting by an old master."*
>
> —Cleveland sportswriter Bill Livingston, after watching Butch Reynolds win the 400 meters at the World Indoor Track and Field Championships

stayed unsullied were it not for his 1910 comeback fight against Jack Johnson, the first black heavyweight champion. The bout was fought under a cloud of racial antagonism, and after Johnson KOed Jeffries, street fighting broke out in several cities.

39. TOM JENKINS—when the Greeks held the Olympics, wrestling was the most popular sport, and Jenkins was the first American to inherit wrestling's ancient and honorable mantle. Having been born in Cleveland, he gave Greco-Roman wrestling an American twist and popularized the freestyle form that allows legs and holds to be used below the waist. Jenkins became the U.S. wrestling champion in 1893 and held the title for 12 years before retiring to a coaching job at West Point, where his apt pupils included Cadet Dwight D. Eisenhower.

40. BOBBY RAHAL—undoubtedly the fastest man Dublin ever produced, race car driver Rahal won the 1986 Indianapolis 500 by traveling at an average speed of 170.722 mph.

41. BUTCH REYNOLDS—the Akron runner who set the 400–meter world record (43.29) in 1988, was barred from competing two years later by the International Amateur Athletic Foundation for using steroids. Saying it wasn't so, Reynolds sued the IAAF and won a moral victory in 1992, when he was awarded $27 million in still-uncollected damages.

42. JESSE OWENS—the Clevelander was the toast of the 1936 Berlin Olympics where he took four gold medals—the 100-meter dash, the 200-meter dash, the 400-meter relay, and the long jump—in a victory that was moral as well as athletic. He, a black American, had with enormous dignity and grace, stolen the Olympics out from under the racist nose of Adolph Hitler. Sadly, Owens's achievements were ignored in his own country by the Amateur Athletic Union, which annually presents its Sullivan Award to America's outstanding amateur athlete. In 1935, when Owens set his slew of new world records, the award went to golfer Lawson Little, and in 1936, it was given to Glenn Morris, who had one Olympic gold medal in the decathalon.

43. EDWIN MOSES—the Dayton track and field star and Sullivan Award winner who earned gold medals in the 400-meter hurdles at both the 1976 and 1984 Olympics. Between 1977 and 1987, he won 122 consecutive races.

44. MIKE SCHMIDT—the Daytonian who was the home run king of the 1980s. In 1987 with the Philadelphia Phillies, he became only the 14th major leaguer to hit 500 home runs.

45. WAITE HOYT—a Yankee during the heady Babe Ruth era of the 1920s, he not only who pitched his way into seven World Series and the Baseball Hall of Fame, but also coined the phrase, "It's great to be young and a Yankee." The glib Hoyt then became one of the first—and best—players turned announcer, pitching a wealth of stories and anecdotes as the "voice of the Cincinnati Reds" on radio for 24 years.

46. HARVEY HADDIX—the Medway native earned a curious place in the annals of baseball history on May 26, 1959, when he became the first major leaguer to pitch—and lose—a perfect game that went into extra innings. Playing for the Pittsburgh Pirates, the southpaw had retired 36 Braves batters during 12 impeccable innings at Milwaukee's County Stadium. But the game turned imperfect for Haddix in the 13th inning, when an error by the Pirates' Don Hoak let the Braves' Felix Mantilla get to first base. Eddie Mathews bunted Mantilla to second, and then Joe Adcock hit the ball over the center field fence, allowing Mantilla to score and the Braves to win, 1–0. The next year, Haddix won two games during the Pirates' Cinderella victory over the New York Yankees in the World Series, and he retired with a 136–113 career record in 1965.

47. JIM BROWN—an All-American at Syracuse University, Brown played with the Cleveland Browns from 1957–1965, a period in which he was simply the best ball carrier in the NFL.

Babe Ruth was probably as well known for his partying and cavorting as for prowess with a bat. When Ruth died in 1948, pitcher Waite Hoyt was one of the pallbearers. It was a scorching August day, and Cardinal Francis Spellman conducted an long, elaborate service. Former Yankee Joe Dugan said to Hoyt, "I'd give a hundred dollars for a beer." Hoyt answered, "So would the Babe."

A four-time Player of the Year who rushed for 1,000 or more yards in seven seasons, he set record after record until retiring at age 29 to try his hand at making movies. Though he hasn't played in almost 30 years, he still is the NFL's all-time leader in touchdowns (126) and in average yards per carry (5.22).

♦ **48. JOHNNY BENCH**—arguably the best player that the Reds have ever had, Bench spent his entire major league career (1967–1983) with Cincinnati. In the 1970s, the big-fisted, hard-hitting catcher virtually redefined the position. Bench had 389 career home runs and was the World Series Most Valuable Player in 1976. In 1989, he became only the thirteenth major league catcher inducted into the Baseball Hall of Fame.

49. OTTO GRAHAM—from 1946–1955, he was Paul Brown's right hand man on the Cleveland Browns team, a superb quarterback blessed with brains, agility, running ability, and an incredible arm that made him one of the finest long ball passers in pro football history. They were a perfect combination: Brown liked to call the plays, and Graham was ready, willing, and able to execute them. Together, they took the Browns to four consecutive All-American Football Conference championships and three NFL championships in ten seasons. Graham was Player of the Year in 1953 and 1955, and his career totals included more than 23,000 yards passing and 174 touchdown passes.

50. DON SHULA—the winningest coach in pro football history was born in Grand River, educated at John Carroll University, and played briefly for the Cleveland Browns before being traded to the Colts and Redskins. Shula cut his coaching teeth with Baltimore, then took over the Miami Dolphins in 1970. A tough-minded and strong-willed disciplinarian, he has taken teams to the Super Bowl six times, gone home to Miami as the champion two times, and been named Coach of the Year four times. Shula hit his winning landmark on November 14, 1993, when he achieved career victory number 325. He not only surpassed the previous record holder George Halas, but also cemented a .678 in total career wins.

◆ BENCHMARKS

SMARTS
Johnny Bench, who studied batters astutely, was a master strategist, the archetypal cerebral catcher, which might explain why his hat size was $7^{1}/_{2}$.

STRENGTH
Bench was one of the premiere power hitters of the 1970s, and over his career hit more home runs than any other catcher.

SIZE
At 6' 1", 200 pounds, Bench gave pitchers a wide target. "When a catcher's wide like that," said one, "he looks a lot closer."

SELF-CONTROL
"The last thing I'll ever do is panic," said Bench.

COMMAND
PERSONALITY
"He'll come out to the mound and chew me out as if I were a two-year-old," said Reds pitcher Jim Maloney, eight years Bench's senior.

ARM
Bench began baseball as a pitcher and some contended he had the strongest arm in the majors. "I wish I could throw like he does, "said one Reds pitcher. "I can throw out any base-runner alive," said Bench. Base-stealers are normally 70% successful. Bench held them under 50%.

VERSATILITY
Bench played six positions in 1970.

LONGEVITY
Bench caught 100 or more games for 13 seasons, tying Bill Dickey's major league mark.

" *There are a few memorable athletes about whom greatness is simply understood. With Bench it was as though he needed only put in the time, that the natural course of events would take him to the station that awaited him from the beginning. 'I want to be remembered as the greatest catcher who ever played,' he said late in his career. 'I wanted that when I was 19 years old.' "*

—Lonnie Wheeler

139

♦ The circumstances occur so rarely that only a handful of pitchers in major league history have been able to strike out four batters in a single inning. Here is what has to happen: the catcher errors on the third strike and the batter advances to first base. Then the pitcher has to strike out another batter.

Number of times Ohio State football teams have claimed the national collegiate championship—3, in 1942, 1954, 1968.

Number of Ohio State football coaches who had national champion teams—2; Paul Brown in 1942, and Woody Hayes in 1954 and 1968

Woody Hayes

Number of Ohio State players leading the team in total yards rushing and receiving in the same year—3; Howard "Hopalong" Cassady, 1954; Ron Springs, 1977; Keith Byars, 1984

Number of Ohio State players leading the team in touchdowns and total yards rushing and receiving in the same year—1, Keith Byars, 1984

Number of major league players on Ohio teams elected to the National Baseball Hall of Fame in their first year of eligibility—4; Cleveland Indians pitcher Bob Feller, 1962; Cincinnati Reds catcher Johnny Bench, 1989; Cincinnati Reds second baseman Joe Morgan, 1990; Cincinnati Reds pitcher Tom Seaver, 1992

Number of first year Cincinnati Reds managers whose teams have finished in first place—4; Patrick Moran, 1919; Sparky Anderson, 1970; John McNamara, 1979; Lou Piniella, 1990

Number of major league players on Ohio teams who have had four home runs in a single game—1, the Cleveland Indians' Rocky Colavito, June 10, 1959

Number of major league players on Ohio teams who have hit 40 or more home runs in a season—8; the Cleveland Indians' Al Rosen in 1953, Hal Trosky in 1936, and Rocky Colavito in 1958 and 1959; the Cincinnati Reds' Ted Kluszewski in 1954, Wally Post in 1955, Tony Perez and Johnny Bench in 1970, George Foster in 1977

♦ *Number of major leaguers on Ohio teams who have struck out four batters in one inning*—7; the Cleveland Indians' Guy Morton in 1916, Lee Strange in 1964, Mike Paxton in 1978, Paul Shuey in 1994; the Cincinnati Reds' Joe Nuxhall in 1959, Mario Soto in 1984, Tim Birtsas in 1990

DOLLAR VALUE OF OHIO'S MAJOR LEAGUE FRANCHISES, ACCORDING TO FINANCIAL WORLD'S 1993 SURVEY

Cleveland Browns—
  $133 million
Cincinnati Bengals—
  $128 million
Cincinnati Reds—
  $103 million
Cleveland Indians—
  $81 million
Cleveland Cavaliers—
  $81 million

Only pro football team that lacks a logo—Cleveland Browns

Only National Football League teams that have never had cheerleaders—the Cleveland Browns, Pittsburgh Steelers, and New York Jets

Elvis Presley's favorite football team—the Cleveland Browns, whose pre-1962 glories captured the King's attention and admiration

Only team to lose a Super Bowl while leading in total yardage—Cincinnati Bengals, which bested San Francisco by 356–275 yards, but lost the 1981 Super Bowl, 26–21

Team that lost the Super Bowl in front of the most people—the 1981 Cincinnati Bengals, who on January 24, 1982, succumbed to the 49ers in front of the 40,020,000 households watching Super Bowl XVI

First Ohio State coach with a football team finishing at the bottom of the Big Ten—Wes Fesler, in 1947

First Miami University football coach to be fired—Tim Rose (31–44–3), 1989

Most quickly fired manager in major league baseball history—Tuscarawas County native Cy Young, who struck out in Boston after only seven games, 1907

Fifth most quickly fired manager in major league history—Tony Perez, cut by Cincinnati after only 44 games, 1993

Team that lost each of the following American League landmark games in 1901: first baseball game, first Sunday game, first doubleheader—Cleveland Indians

First major league team with three pitchers winning 20 games as well as the league leaders in home runs and RBIs that did not win a pennant—1952 Cleveland Indians

*Major league team that won a record-setting 111 games in 1954, then got blanked in the World Series—*1954 Cleveland Indians, who were swept in the Series's first four games by the New York Giants

*Only major league team to sandwich a winning season between two 100-loss seasons—*Cleveland Indians, who went 60–102 in 1985; 84–78 in 1986; and 61–101 in 1987

*Most stolen bases permitted by a catcher in a single American League game—*13, by New York Yankee and Pike County native Branch Rickey, June 28, 1907

*First major league team to lose a game at the Baltimore Orioles' new Camden Yards park—*Cleveland Indians, 1992

*Smallest U.S. city with a major league franchise—*Cincinnati, population 364,040

*Only major league teams that did not set a new single-season attendance record in the 1980s—*Cleveland and Seattle

*National Basketball Association team with the most consecutive losses—*the Cleveland Cavaliers, who lost 24 games in a row (19 at the end of the 1981–1982 season plus 5 at the start of the 1982–1983 season) between March 19, 1982 and November 10, 1982

*First coach fired by George Steinbrenner—*John McLendon, who went to work for the fickle George Steinbrenner as coach of the American Basketball League's Cleveland Pipers in 1961.

*First team to be the runner-up in a National Collegiate Athletic Association Division I basketball championship—*Ohio State, defeated by Oregon 46–33 in 1939

*Major league pitcher with the second longest string of consecutive losses—*Delaware native Clifton Curtis's ill-fated 23-game streak, 1910–1911

> "I told him there were two areas of the city he doesn't belong in, the bench and the locker room."
>
> —John McLendon about George Steinbrenner

Ohio Machismo. Think there's no such thing? Think again. We didn't invent it. But we almost did. Call it "machio". The thermometer read -9 in Cincinnati just before kick-off at the 1981 AFC play-offs between the Bengals and the frost-shocked San Diego Chargers. The Chargers came out swaddled to the eyebrows in thermal underwear, mittens, caps, scarves, earmuffs, bench coats and electric footwarmers. Anthony Munoz and his Bengal teammates came out bare-armed for what turned out to be a cold day in hell for the Chargers. Some Bengal fans (all male) came out bare-chested. The game went down in history as the Freezer Bowl; they should have called it the Macho Cup. Hemingway defined courage as grace under pressure. The Ohio variety of macho can be described as grace under posture. Sheer aggression or pigheaded willfulness is not enough. There must be additional elements, not only of style but of calculation behind the strutting. True macho also requires a dash of childish geewhiz to go with the blood, sweat and boorishness. Woody Hayes is the greatest modern definition of the Macho Ohio Man. He ended his career by slugging a fully-armored player on national television, which certainly has the macho ethos at heart—make the gesture; blast the consequences. But Woody usually carried his grace well, preaching pain and effort as a way to salvation, not merely to success. Macho can intoxicate grown men and women, leading to spectacularly foolish acts with dreadful consequences. It lures men onto steep rooftops where they have no business and women into carrying heavy objects best left behind. For good or ill, Ohio Machismo is a force to be reckoned with, as any motorist who has ever tried to merge onto a stalled interstate will testify. We are prejudiced because we see it largely as a positive thing, the manifestation of a deeply Ohioan impulse toward contrarianism. Spit in the eye of the sensible thing. Root hard or die. In this rosy view, when Ohio macho goes awry or turns malacious, it is no longer the true spirit but a demented mutation. If you don't agree, you're probably in the grip of the macho molecules yourself. And if you want to make something of it, just step across this paragraph.

℞

MEN WITH BALLS

HOMBRE. Woody Hayes would take on anything: cameramen, players, writers, fans, yard markers—he'd even punch himself. He was the toughest coach in football. When frustration in the 1978 Gator Bowl aided Woody in punching Clemson's nose guard, he knocked himself out of football. Afterward, he offered no half-cocked rationales. Wrote one perceptive writer, "He thus spared himself the impossible task of explaining how it feels to be a man at war with something like time."

PLUCK. In 1992, against Miami in a smashing Monday night game and an astoundingly literal application of not having a leg to stand on, Cleveland QB Bernie Kosar showed true grit—he broke his ankle and still rallied the Browns from a 20–3 fourth-quarter deficit to a 23–20 lead. So Dan Marino drove 84 yards for the win. There wasn't a dry throat in the house, anyway.

HARDNOSE. Bengal nose tackle Tim Krumrie broke his leg in three places in the 1989 Super Bowl but refused treatment until late in the game. He propped himself up in the training room and watched his teammates on television. His pre-game frenzies are legendary and so are his training camp skirmishes with teammates. Sometimes, he spits on the ball to disrupt the center's attention. Once, he dislocated three fingers on one play and reset them himself without missing a down. Twice All-Pro, he now plays with a metal rod in his leg, and once said, "There's nothing like a good collision."

"Now go back to the Battle of Salamis, where the Greeks beat the tail off the Persians. Now doesn't that take in so many of the things used in football: fear, determination, backs to the wall, home field advantage—all the things you see in a football game . . ."

—Woody Hayes

HEAD MAN. The Cleveland Browns' Ron Wolfley was a four-time Pro Bowler whose entire career has been based largely upon his calling as special teams kamikaze. He's the talent who led the kickoff charge downfield, breaking up the blocking, and he was the best in the business. Said his agent: "If you gave Ron a choice between taking big money and knocking a guy into a snot bubble, he'll take knocking a guy into a snot bubble." Said Wolfley: "Humongous collisions. Enormous, monstrous collisions."

ARTS AND CRAFTS. Chris Spielman revealed the essence of the linebacker's art by tackling his grandmother when he was five years old. Said he: "She went to give me a hug, and I took her out. I knocked her down, but she bounced back up. You could tell she was a Spielman." What big hams you have, Grannie.

DON LOOK BACK. Don Zimmer of Cincinnati's West Side was "frighteningly beaned" in a Columbus, Ohio, 1954 minor-league game. He stuttered for a year but returned to play and in 1956, his head still in the game, had his cheekbone broken with another pitch. That 1954 pitch brought about the mandatory batting helmet.

TRAINMAN'S HEADACHE. "My idea of a good hit is when the victim wakes up on the sidelines with train whistles blowing in his head," said Jack Tatum, OSU's All-American safety. By the time he finished OSU he had, by his own admission, more knockouts than Muhammad Ali. At Oakland, they called him The Assassin. Darryl Stingley would probably agree.

SUPER JOE. Joe Charboneau, a Cleveland Indian in 1980, was the prototypical wild man. Joe ate lit cigarettes, drank beer through his nose, pulled one of his own teeth with a pair of pliers, and once sewed up a cut on his arm with fishing line. "Things just happen to me," he said. He finished the year as the American League Rookie of the Year, which was one of the few normal things that ever happened to him.

PLATE TECTONICS. Jimmie Wilson was 40 years old when he became the hero of the 1940 World Series. A Cincinnati Reds coach, he went behind the plate after Willard Hershberger's suicide. After playing, he went to his room and soaked his muscles in Epsom salts. Wrote one reporter, "The archaic catcher finished Monday's game with a veritable stable of charley-horses. His legs looked like gunny-sacks of squash." But Wilson caught six of the seven games, fielded perfectly, and hit .353.

Chris Spielman

Pam Postema

WOMEN WITH BALLS

THE UMPIRE STRIKES BACK. Pam Postema, tomboy daughter of a Willard vegetable farmer, umpired the first Triple A All-Star game but never got into The Show. One of her confreres said she was good enough "if only she had outdoor plumbing." At a Columbus Clippers game, when three OSU students heckled her about her chest size, she said to startled manager Bucky Dent, "How dare they say I have no ****?" She called Lenny Dykstra "a miserable little puke," and, all-in-all, gave as good as she got. Pam, bam, thank you, ma'am.

LOCAL HEAT. Alta Weiss, of Ragersville, Ohio, was a cigar-smoking, spit-balling tomboy with a medical degree. The largest contradiction, however, was her ability to beat men at their own game—baseball. She had a man's windup, good speed and, in 1907 when she was 17 and playing against the semipro Vermilion Independents, she struck out 15 men. She also re-defined the taunt, "You throw like a girl," into a compliment.

MYTHFITS

TO DIE AS ONE LIVED. Mike Fink, Ohio River keelboatman, was, at one time, a *real* man, even though he said he was half horse, half alligator, and could lick all comers, man or beast. The evidence seems to be that he probably could and may have. Even before the legend, Mike was the quintessential roughneck in a frontier world of roughnecks. When he died in a fight over a woman in 1823, he was just beginning to live.

IN YOUR FACE. The sport of gouging, imported from England, reached the height of its popularity in the Ohio River Valley during the early 1800s. Equipment requirement: one long and sharp thumbnail, used to to gouge out an opponent's eyeball. Lots of testosterone all around; one-eyed Jacks wild.

> *" The key to success is a good eye, an even temper, and being the boss of your game. You should also know where the nearest exit is. And remember to tell the score-keeper where you want the body sent."*
>
> —*Pam Postema*

MERCENARIES

COOL HAND, KEEN EYE. The Cincinnati Kid, in the novel by the same name, takes on dead-eyed Lancey Hodges in a stud game that begins on page 84 and doesn't end until page 140. It's one of sport's classic *mano-a-mano* faceoffs. Even those who know nothing about poker walk away in a wilt.

MAN AT WORK. Mandingo, a real stud, has fathered more than 45,000 offspring. He's a history-making legend at Plain City's Select Sires, the world's largest producer of bull semen. Mandingo gives at the office three days a week and, according to the company newsletter, "continues to satisfy dairymen around the world." And, obviously, their charges. Unfortunately, his job is a little artificial; Mandingo has never, in the biblical sense, known a cow.

HARDCASES

TRADITION. OSU running back, Robert Smith: "Personally, I don't give a s— what Woody Hayes said."

POSITION. Reds manager Pete Rose in 1987 assailing his players for making excuses: "I was served with divorce papers and a paternity suit and went 17 for 28."

PREMONITION. Joseph Csonka of Stowe, Ohio, explaining his son's football attitude: "I remember hearing the dog bark, going outside and seeing three-year-old Larry with one of the dog's legs in his mouth. I asked him what he was doing and he said, 'He bit me first.'"

EXPECTATION. Earle Bruce, describing how Buckeye fans liked the OSU coach: "Undefeated, or dead."

HEAVYWEIGHTS

BIG STICK. Ted Kluszewski, Cincinnati's great power slugger, led the majors in 1954 with 49 homers. He weighed 240, with massive arms that left legions of female fans swooning in the bleachers. The defense swooned in the outfield.

BIG LICK. They staged a bayonet drill in the ring before the 1919 Jack Dempsey–Jess Willard championship fight in Toledo. The fight itself was at 3:30 on the afternoon of July 4th. It was said to be 101 under an umbrella. Were Dempsey's hands wrapped with plaster of paris and larceny? His right broke Willard's cheekbone in the first round, when Willard went down seven times. He broke Willard's ribs in the second round. He outweighed Dempsey by 58 pounds and never had a chance. Jimmy Breslin said the Roaring Twenties began in Toledo that day. The crowd was drinking the nation's first illegal hootch. Too bad Willard wasn't.

STREETFIGHTERS

JUMPSTART. Sam Brady, Army scout and Ohio's first real track and field man, led hostile Indians on a hundred-mile chase across Ohio in 1780, very nearly coming to a dead end at the Cuyahoga River. He saved his skin with a daring 22-foot jump across the river gorge, marking one of Ohio's earliest examples of how motivation tools could be used in athletic performances.

SCHOOL OF HARD JOCKS. Paul Newman, movie actor late of Shaker Heights, was kicked off the Kenyon College JV football team for brawling. Say it ain't so, Paul.

PALOOKAS

EARSHOT. Don King, on his way to fame as a boxing promoter, made a name for himself first as a Cleveland numbers operator. Called to testify in an extortion trial, King was hit in the back of the head with a shotgun blast that "blew holes in his ears big enough to see through." He was hurt but not enough to keep him from testifying.

BANTAMWEIGHTS. In 1991, Ohio Supreme Court Justice Craig Wright grabbed Ohio Supreme Court justice Andrew Douglas, threw him into a desk, and jumped him until court workers sent them to neutral corners. Shining example of macho juris imprudence.

Opening scene, The Last Boy Scout, 1991: "Open the holes up! Get in there like hogs, like pigs! Kick some butt! Let's get out of this town as a winner! I hate Cleveland!"

"I'd rather go out with my ex-wife's attorney than play
in the minor leagues."
—*Dave Collins, Cincinnati Reds outfielder*

"They've never been on a baseball field. Anybody can play
ball in a saloon."
—*Fred Hutchinson, Reds manager, on armchair managers*

"I need cortisone for both knees. I take butazolidin, endizine,
and muscle relaxer. If I were a race horse, I would be
disqualified."
—*Johnny Bench, Cincinnati Reds catcher, 1981*

"Gates, I'm sure some of our students would be interested
to know—what did you take when you were in school?"
"Overcoats, mostly."
—*exchange between Detroit pitcher Gates Brown (who
was discovered while doing time in the Mansfield State
Reformatory for breaking and entering) and the principal
of Brown's high school in Crestline, Ohio*

"I didn't try too hard. I was afraid I'd get emotionally involved
with the cow."
—*Rocky Bridges, Reds infielder, on finishing second
in a Fans' Appreciation Night cow-milking contest*

"God doesn't care about us. If he did, Billy Graham would
hit .400."
—*Chris Sabo, Reds third baseman*

"I only gave up three runs—Rosie gets half of everything."
—*Jose Rijo, Reds pitcher, in the midst of divorce proceed-
ings, after allowing six runs in an exhibition game*

Reporter: "Would you rather face Jim Palmer or Tom Seaver?"
Merv Rettennund, Reds outfielder: "That's like asking me if I'd
rather be hung or go to the electric chair."

"When you play this game 20 years, go to bat 10,000 times, and get 3,000 hits, do you know what that means? You've gone 0 for 7,000."
    —Pete Rose

"I got the sophomore jinx out of the way and I think I'll have my best year ever next year. There's no junior jinx, is there?"
    —Joe Charboneau, Cleveland Indians

"It's called a nudist ball; it's got nothing on it."
    —Phil Hennigan, Cleveland Indians pitcher

"Watching Pat Corrales signal for a reliever is like watching a guy with no money in his pocket reach for a restaurant check, desperately hoping somebody will come along and save him."
    —sportswriter Moss Klien, on the Cleveland Indians 1987 bullpen

"What was wrong with it?"
"It sounded a little high."
    —dialogue between umpire and Mike Kreevich of the White Sox, protesting a Bob Feller strike call

"It starts out like a baseball and when it gets to the plate it looks like a marble."
"You must be talkin' about my slow ball. My fastball looks like a fish egg."
    —dialogue between hitter Hack Wilson and pitcher Satchel Paige

"The weather's cold. My club's bad. My knee hurts. I can't putt no more. I'm off my diet. My wife is nagging me. Other than that, everything's great."
    —Cincinnatian Don Zimmer, managing the Chicago Cubs

When Miami University pulled off a surprise upset of No. 3-ranked Louisiana State in 1986, Louisiana field goal kicker Ronnie Lewis expressed his opinion of the 21–12 score by holding up one strategic finger on both hands as he left the field. More than a few people took offense, but one sympathizer allowed that Lewis probably didn't mean anything obscene and was just trying to convey "We're No. 11."

"The goal line is north and south. The cheerleaders are east and west. Please don't get the two confused."
—Coach Vince Suriano, Cincinnati Anderson High School, advice to his running backs

"For years the Bengals drafted kids that looked like Tarzan and played like Jane."
—Cris Collinsworth, ex-Bengal receiver and radio/TV commentator

"The drop is everything. Timing is everything. Everything is everything."
—Bengal Lee Johnson, explaining the secrets of punting

"I don't have a bad memory from my 13 years. Come to think of it, I don't have a memory at all."
—Al (Bubba) Baker, Cleveland defensive end, upon retiring

"When I came here, I signed a non-aggression pact."
—Lou Holtz, on lettering only one year as linebacker at Kent State

"Life without football is not life."
—motto under senior yearbook picture of Jerry Glanville, Perrysburg, Ohio, High School 1959 Yearbook

"We are starting from scratch. These days our staff meetings are very brief. Head coach Pont asks offensive coordinator Pont and defensive coordinator Pont if they want to have a staff meeting and when both say, 'No,' we are out of there."
—John Pont, as he organized the first football team for the College of Mount St. Joseph in Cincinnati, 1989

"If getting hit is a God-given talent, I guess I have it."
—Tom Waddle, Chicago Bears wide receiver (Cincinnati Moeller High)

"When the crowd started chanting, 'Dino, Dino,'
his parents must have felt five feet tall."
  —*Dave Graf, Cleveland linebacker, on an ovation for
  teammate Dino Hall, who is 5'7"*

"Well, we do have a draw play."
  —*Pat McInally, Bengal punter, when asked if art history
  courses he took at Harvard helped him in the NFL*

"They fortunately send a lot of guys to medical school, whom I
will be calling upon after my career is over."
  —*Bengal linebacker Reggie Williams, one of only three
  Dartmouth grads in the NFL, commenting on his alma mater*

"I don't think any kid ever looks back between his legs and says,
'Some day, I'm going to do this in the Super Bowl.'"
  —*Ed Brady, Cincinnati Bengals' long snapper*

"The hardest thing about prize fightin' is pickin' up yer teeth
with a boxing glove on."
  —*Ohio humorist Kin Hubbard*

"If you drink, don't drive. Don't even putt."
  —*Steubenville's Dean Martin*

"It caught me in the worst possible place, coach—the palms
of my hands."
  —*Ohio State's Jerry Lucas, explaining why he dropped
  the basketball*

"We're the only team in history that could lose nine games in
a row and then go into a slump."
  —*Bill Fitch, Cleveland Cavaliers coach*

"The only difference between Cleveland and the *Titanic*
is that the *Titanic* had better restaurants.
—*sportswriter Barney Nagler*

"If you're going to have a plane crash in Cleveland,
it's better to have one on the way in than on the way out."
—*sportswriter Peter Gammons*

"It was too bad I wasn't a second baseman; then I'd probably
have seen a lot more of my husband."
—*Karolyn Rose on ex-husband Pete*

"All of us learn to write in the second grade . . . most of us
go on to greater things."
—*Massillon native and University of Indiana basketball
coach Bobby Knight*

"I go to the park sick as a dog, and when I see my uniform
hanging there I get well right now. Then I see some of the
guys and I get sick again."
—*Pete Rose, on the press*

"Last year wasn't all that bad. We led the league in flu shots."
—*Bill Fitch, Cleveland Cavaliers coach*

"The more things change, they more they don't. In 1992, as
in 1967, the only thing you absolutely need to be a Cincinnati
Red is a razor. The last Red to have facial hair was Stalin.
He's dead."
—*Paul Daugherty, Cincinnati Post columnist*

"Knowing all about baseball is just about as profitable as being
a good whittler."
—*Kin Hubbard, Ohio humorist*

"Cincinnati is nuts with baseball! They ought to call this town Cincinnutty!"
—*sportswriter Bugs Baer, after the Reds won the 1919 World Series*

"The truth is, so many jocks now belong to the 'I just give it 110 percent school,' it's almost not worth talking to them. If cliches were raindrops, every sportswriter's day would be London."
—*Paul Daugherty, Cincinnati Post*

"The As leave after this game for Cleveland. It was only by a 13–12 vote that they decided to go."
—*Lon Simmons, Oakland A's announcer, 1982*

"How could it have been a perfect game? It was in Cleveland."
—*Randy Galloway, sportswriter, on Indians pitcher Len Barker throwing a perfect game against Toronto, May 15, 1981*

"Free admission to anyone who was actually alive the last time the Indians won the pennant."
—*Cleveland announcer in the movie, Major League*

"Davis, Eric, OF. Great speed and power, outstanding outfielder. Led the league in homers, RBIs, fielding percentage, aches, pains, athletic tape, knee braces, liniment and rubdowns. Voted MVP by the league's trainers, narrowly edging stunt men and train wrecks."
—*Paul Daugherty, Cincinnati Post, on Eric Davis's fragile frame, April 26, 1991*

"When Dibble's head catches up with his arm, he'll really have something."
    —Paul Daugherty, Cincinati Post, April 23, 1991,
    (after Ron Dibble was fined $1,000 and suspended three days
    for throwing a fastball behind Astro shortstop Eric Yelding)

"Now that Charlie Finley and his jackass Charlie O. are retired from the game, Schott is the only mogul of either gender who would appear in public trailed by a large animal of unknown purpose."
    —Dave Kindred, National Sports Daily, October 18, 1990

"The Reds are owned by a fiesty lady who puts the stadium ushers in tuxedos and tried to put her ballplayers in doggy ears, so help me."
    —Art Spander, San Francisco Chronicle

"Working for George Steinbrenner is like working for Ivan the Terrible, only the hours are longer."
    —Paul Daugherty, Cincinnati Magazine

"Saying Rose got kicked out of baseball for associating with gamblers is like saying the *Titanic* sank from associating with icebergs."
    —Rick Reilly, Sports Illustrated, August 16, 1993

"Umpires operate under one prevailing notion: They are always right. In fact, they're pretty much perfect. They've never made one mistake in their entire umpiring lives. They thought they did once, but they were wrong. That was a long time ago."
    —Paul Daugherty, Cincinnati Post, August 24, 1991

"Cincinnatians can understand a tight end dropping a pass. They just can't understand why he still gets paid after dropping it."
    —Mark Purdy, on unforgiving sports fans

"New England was so bogged down offensively that next week they may consider commissioning a still-life portrait rather than go to the expense of game films."
 —*Tim Sullivan, Cincinnati Enquirer columnist, after the Bengals' 20–10 win, December 21, 1992*

"A body only an embalmer could love."
 —*sports writer Bill Livingston, on Carl "Big Daddy" Hairston, 1990*

"I've had loose change move around in the pocket better than Bernie."
 —*Tom Zenner, Omaha sportscaster, on Bernie Kosar's mobility, Sports Illustrated, November 8, 1993*

"What's that bird-chested bastard doing wearing an O? What did he *do* to get it? What *could* he do?
 —*OSU football coach Francis Schmidt, who thought only big guys should be awarded varsity O's*

"I am always perversely pleased when that many people can be disappointed all at once."
 —*overheard, after Michigan beat undefeated OSU, November 20, 1993*

"Both teams treated the ball as if it were a bouquet of poison ivy."
 —*John McNulty, on the 1950 OSU–Michigan Blizzard Bowl, The New Yorker, December 16, 1950*

Punter to John Heisman: "Coach, do you know that they call this toe on my right foot 'the million dollar toe?'"
Heisman to punter: "What good is it if you only have a fifteen-cent head?"

A Subjective List of the Most Legendary Ohio State Basketballers

1. GEORGE BELLOWS (1903–04)—The famous painter got his start as an OSU hoopster whose career included a 16-point performance in an 88–2 win over Ohio University; went on to make All-Realist team.

2. LYNN W. ST. JOHN (1912–19)—Only had a 79–69 record at OSU but as athletic director from 1915–47, he legitimized and lengthened the basketball schedule. He also pushed for formal codification of international basketball rules and helped quell splits among amateur basketball factions in the Olympics. He was also elected to the Naismith Memorial Basketball Hall of Fame.

3. CHARLES "SHIFTY" BOLEN (1916–18)—The captain of the 1918 team, claiming it brought him good luck, slept in a bed with coffin handles on the side and a pewter plate mounted about his head that read "At Rest."

4. HAROLD G. OLSEN (1923–46)—Accumulated a 255–192 record as coach, and led the committee that created the NCAA Tournament in which he coached OSU in the first championship finals.

5. JOHNNY MINER (1923–25)—Not one of OSU coach George Trautman's favorites, Miner didn't make the team his first year but new coach Olsen discovered him playing intramurals. Miner went on to become an All-American who led Ohio State to its first Big Ten crown.

6. JIMMY HULL (1936–39)—Greenfield McLain's most illustrious graduate was headed for USC but came down with appendicitis. Deciding that California was too far from home for a recovering appendicitis patient, he ended up at OSU where as a first team All-American led his team to the first NCAA tournament finals.

7. ROBIN FREEMAN (1954–56)—OSU's all-time leading average scorer at 28 points per game, he introduced and perfected the overhead jump shot. If he had played with today's 19' 9" three-point line, he would have completely re-written the record books.

8. JOHN HAVLICEK (1959–61)—A tenacious defender, opposing schools' press releases began noting how many points their stars had been able to score against Havlicek (and, as he noted, his substitutes). After being cut in the final round by the Cleveland Browns football team, he went on to play in 1,270 NBA games for the Boston Celtics.

"*My father, Frank Havlicek, had come to the United States from Czechoslovakia in 1913. He used to tell a story about being given a banana and not even knowing what it was.*"

—*John Havlicek*

9. JERRY LUCAS (1959–61)—The Middletown student-athlete received over 150 scholarship offers before choosing OSU, where the Bucks led the nation in team offense—90.4 points per game—and won the national title his sophomore year. He and Havlicek lost six games in three years, and never at home.

10. GARY BRADDS (1962–64)—After spending a year in Lucas's formidable shadow, Bradds exploded for almost 30 points per game, including a string of six straight games in which he scored over 40 points each. Lucas later said that the best player he competed against in college had been Bradds in practice.

11. JIM CLEAMONS (1969–71)—He scored 1,335 points but his greatest contribution was his leadership, taking a greatly inexperienced team to the 1971 Big Ten title. Fred Taylor said Cleamons, Lucas, and Havlicek were the players who contributed most to OSU basketball.

12. ALLAN HORNYAK (1971–73)—Hornyak once had his scholarship offer removed after he and a friend passed up a recruitment dinner with Fred Taylor to play in a pick-up basketball game. He later regained it and went on to be an All-American who ranked third on OSU's all-time scoring average list.

13. KELVIN RANSEY (1977–80)—The epitome of the point guard, he was an All-American who handed out 516 career assists and came up with 147 steals. With his 827 career field goals, he was the prototype for a future Toledo Macomber High School and OSU player—Jim Jackson.

14. DENNIS HOPSON (1984–87)—OSU's all-time leading scorer with 2,096 points, Hopson was an all-around player among the career leaders for steals, blocked shots, free throws, and three-point shots made—despite only having the shot available to him for one year.

15. JAY BURSON (1986–89)—Entering OSU as Ohio's prep scoring leader, he showed he wasn't too frail for Big Ten play by scoring 1,756 points and snagging 204 steals. Career ended early when his neck was broken during a harsh foul. The standing ovation he received when he first returned courtside—complete with halo brace—was one of the longest of recent memory.

16. JIM JACKSON (1990–92)—With his all-around ability, he returned OSU to national prominence. The collective spirit of OSU basketball fans plunged when he tearfully announced he would forgo his senior year for the riches of the NBA.

TWO LEGENDARY GAMES:

Plus. In 1991, battling for first place in the Big Ten, the Hoosiers came into Columbus and see-sawed back and forth for forty minutes before a hanging, leaning, fifteen-foot shot by Jim Jackson sent the game into overtime. First OT deadlocked. With just over a 12 seconds left in the second OT, score tied at 95, Jackson slipped a pass to Treg Lee whose five-foot jump shot ended one of the greatest games ever played in St. John Arena.

Minus. In 1972, OSU near the top of the national rankings and playing Minnesota away, the Golden Gophers go Golden Gloves, beating up Luke Witte in a game-ending brawl that featured fans coming out of the stands to join in. The shaken Buckeyes shrugged their way through the rest of the season.

"Burson was the people's choice, a daring over-achiever who made beautiful music from a scrawny and ungainly bodily instrument."

—*Cleveland columnist Bill Livingston on Jay Burson*

BYGONE GLORIES:

In the beginning, *Earl "Red" Blaik* created a good name for Miami out of nothingness on the national fields of play. A Daytonian who lettered for the Redskins in their winning years of 1915–1917, Blaik coached at Dartmouth from 1934–1940, then spent 17 remarkable seasons at Army, where he had consecutive national championships in 1944 and 1945, was named the 1946 Coach of the Year, and begat three Heisman Trophy winners: Felix Blanchard, Glenn Davis, and Pete Dawkins. In 1958, Blaik saw that it was good and rested from his labors with a 166–48–14 career record.

Miami then begat *Paul Brown*, a letterman in 1928 and 1929, who coached Ohio State to a national championship in 1942. Brown went to the pros in 1946, and his Cleveland Browns won National Football League championships in 1950, 1954, and 1955. Bedeviled by owner Art Modell, Brown forsook Cleveland and journeyed to Cincinnati, where he created a 100-yard kingdom of his own known as the Bengals. In 1973, Brown saw that it was good, and he rested from his labors with a 222–113–9 career record and a 1967 place in the Pro Football Hall of Fame.

In the 1920s and 1930s, Miami also begat *Wilbur "Weeb" Ewbank* and *Walter "Smokey" Alston*. Ewbank, a football letterman in 1927, became the only man to mold as well as coach both a National Football League and an American Football League team into pro football champions. Ewbank tamed Johnny Unitas and the Baltimore Colts into winning the 1958 and 1959 NFL titles, and in one of pro football's all-time great upsets, he propelled Joe Namath and the New York Jets to victory over the heavily-favored Colts in Super Bowl III. In 1973, Ewbank saw that it was good and rested from his coaching labors with a 102–83–3 career record. He was called to the Pro Football Hall of Fame in 1978. Alston played Miami

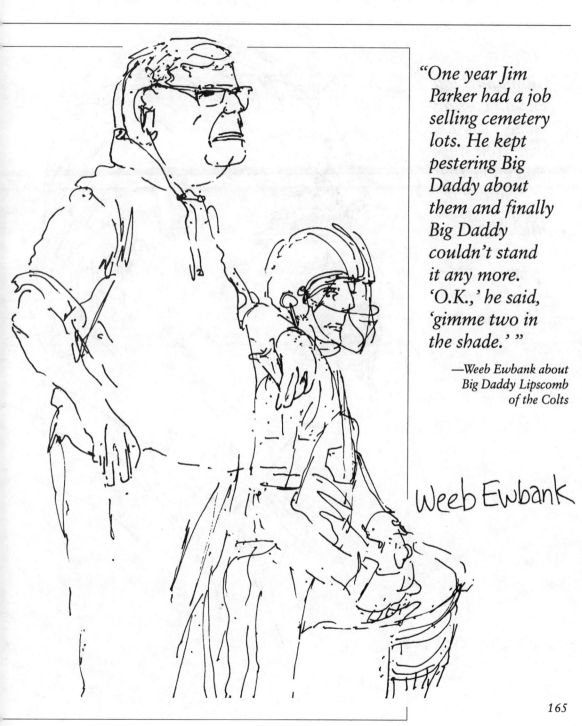

"One year Jim Parker had a job selling cemetery lots. He kept pestering Big Daddy about them and finally Big Daddy couldn't stand it any more. 'O.K.,' he said, 'gimme two in the shade.'"

—Weeb Ewbank about Big Daddy Lipscomb of the Colts

Weeb Ewbank

Gillman: "How can you possibly make a call like that? You stink, you know that, you stink."

Official, walking off a 15-yard penalty: "Hey, Sid, how do I smell from here?"

Sid Gillman

baseball and basketball in the 1930s. As a St. Louis Cardinal in 1936, he struck out in his only time at bat in the major leagues, but he did very well as a minor league baseball coach in Montreal. Alston became manager of the Brooklyn Dodgers in 1954, and the very next year, coached them to the World Series, where they dispatched the Yankees in seven games. Alston managed the Brooklyn-LA Dodgers from 1954–1976, and only two other major league coaches—John McGraw of the New York Giants and Connie Mack of the Philadelphia Athletics—spent more time with a single team. His Dodgers won seven pennants and four World Series (1955, 1959, 1963, 1965). Alston became only the sixth manager in major league history to win 2,000 games, and he was named Manager of the Year in 1955, 1959, and 1963. Seeing that it was good, Alston retired from his labors in 1976 and was elevated to the Baseball Hall of Fame in 1983.

YESTERDAY'S HEROES:

In 1943, Miami's coaching cradle really began to rock with the arrival of *Stu Holcomb*, who was the first in a string of football coaches whose winning Redskins records extended over four decades. Holcomb's team went 7–2–1, and then he moved on to Purdue. *Sid Gillman*, who had been a letterman in the land of the Buckeyes, came to lead the Redskins in 1944. He coached four seasons at Miami, won .829 of his games, and begat an All-American center named *Paul Dietzel* and a half-back called *Ara Parseghian* who helped him win the 1948 Sun Bowl. In 1958, Dietzel would become Coach of the Year for his good works at Louisiana State University, and six years later, Parseghian would get the same honor for his even better work at Notre Dame. Gillman saw that it was good when Miami shaded Texas Tech in the Sun Bowl. Instead of resting, he left for West Point to join the Army under head coach *Earl "Red" Blaik*, who of course just happened to have played football at

"*Motivation. It is, quite simply, the spark that makes someone do that which he might not otherwise do.*"

—Bo Schembechler

Bo Schembechler

Miami. From Army, Gillman went to the University of Cincinnati and then jumped to the pros to coach the Los Angeles Rams and the Los Angeles–San Diego Chargers. Gillman created the wide open offense, formed Los Angeles into the American Football League champions in 1963, and joined the immortals in the Hall of Fame in 1983.

Two seasons after Gillman, *Woody Hayes* arrived to lead the Redskins in their charge toward the 1951 Salad Bowl, the Arizona classic that has since taken on the more appetizing name of Fiesta Bowl. Hayes labored two years at Miami, where he begat seven remarkable Redskins: defensive back *Carmen Cozza*, who went Ivy League and coached football at Yale; *John McVay*, the general manager of the San Francisco 49ers; halfback *John Pont*, who won Coach of the Year honors at Indiana in 1967; quarterback *Jim Root*, who won College Division Coach of the Year honors at New Hampshire in 1967; offensive tackle *Bo Schembechler*, who won Coach of the Year honors at the University of Michigan in 1969; and *Norbert "Nobby" Wirkowski*, who became athletic director at York University in Canada. Hayes saw that it was good when Miami chopped up Arizona in the Salad Bowl. But instead of resting, Hayes left for Ohio State, won the Rose Bowl four times, and compiled a 238–72–10 career record.

After Hayes, Miami's second generation returned to claim their heritage as the Redskins' football chiefs. Akron's *Ara Parseghian*, Class of 1947, was the first of these alumni-turned-coaches. He labored

Miami enjoyed an unsurpassed football season in 1959, when five sons of Oxford headed not only three of the nation's four best college teams (Paul Dietzel at Louisiana State, Red Blaik at Army, and Ara Parseghian at Northwestern), but also the two top-ranked pro teams (Paul Brown at the Cleveland Browns and Weeb Ewbank at the Baltimore Colts).

169

five seasons for a 39–6–1 record, and then went on to Northwestern and Notre Dame, where he had two national collegiate championships. *John Pont* came back to Miami in 1956 and compiled a 43–22–2 tally before leaving for Yale, Indiana, and Northwestern. Barberton's *Bo Schembechler* led the Redskins from 1963–1968 and had a 40–17–3 record. He then advanced to the Big Ten, and from 1969–1989, took the Michigan Wolverines to ten Rose Bowls, two of which they won. Schembechler rested from his labors with a 234–65–8 career record that made him the fifth-winningest National Collegiate Athletic Association Division I coach in college football history.

Parseghian begat *John McVay*, a 1950–1952 Miami letterman, who coached at the University of Dayton from 1964–1971, then joined the New York Giants in 1976. Parseghian and Pont both begat *Bill Mallory*, a Miami alum who took charge of the Redskins in 1969. He had six seasons and a 39–12 record before going to Colorado and Indiana. *Dick Crum* succeeded Mallory, went 34–10–1 in four seasons, then went to North Carolina. Under Mallory and Crum, the Redskins made three consecutive Tangerine Bowl appearances in 1973, 1974, and 1975, and silenced some of the biggest guns in the South—Florida, Georgia, and South Carolina.

THE BEAT GOES ON:
Miami begat its third generation with coach *Randy Walker*, who played tailback-wingback-fullback on the Redskins teams of the Tangerine Bowl era. Walker was an assistant coach at Miami, North Carolina, and Northwestern before he became the Redskins head coach in 1990. With a 17–13–3 record in his first three years, he has yet to rest from the labor of leading the Redskins to future gridiron glories.

NATIVE SON

Walter Alston was a big Ohio farmboy who won seven pennants on both coasts with the Dodgers, yet couldn't wait to return home to Darrtown, a little community just northwest of Cincinnati where he lived across the street from his parents and spent his winters hanging around the hardware store, shooting pool, and watching Miami University basketball games. If Alston preferred the bucolic Cincinnati countryside to the coastal lights, he was anything but unsophisticated on the playing field. He was not a gifted player, and through most of his minor league career he taught high school on the side, coming into the Dodger system by way of another Ohioan, Branch Rickey. He didn't disappoint Rickey, going on to win 2,040 games over 23 games, along with four World Series. Only four other managers won more. Alston was known for his patient, straight-arrow, team-oriented approach. Alston's psychology was that of the Ohio work ethic, a bit dour, with one careful eye always on the horizon, and his background was the kind that allowed him to be found helping his equipment manager pack the team trunk. When his Dodgers won their third World Series in a decade, one of the major celebrations was in an unlikely place—back in little Darrtown, Ohio, which exploded in uncharacteristic fervor.

Walter Alston practiced his pitches by throwing them against the side of his father's barn. He got his nickname while growing up in Butler County, where he was said to hurl his fastball so hard that it smoked. "I lost the fastball before I got old enough for it to do me any good," Alston later allowed, "and since I could hit, I became a first baseman."

THESE DIAMONDS ARE FOREVER

Eleven Ohio baseball players whose sparkle was among the best and brightest

Of all the statistical benchmarks that baseball uses to measure greatness, the most precious are attaining a .400 single season batting average and pitching a perfect game. The rarefied ratio that compares the number-of-hits to times-at-bat has been achieved by only nine major league players, five of whom were either from Ohio or lent their skills to Ohio teams. Similarly, the perfect game, in which there are no hits and no runs and no batter reaches first base (not even for a walk) during nine complete innings of play, has been executed and won by only a dozen major league pitchers, six of whom were Ohioans or associated with Ohio teams.

THE .400 HITTERS:

GEORGE SISLER

Born in Manchester (Stark County), Ohio, in 1893, Sisler was an extraordinary first baseman and a consistently fine hitter. Except for the brief stint with the Boston Braves, his career from 1915–1936 was spent with the St. Louis Browns as a player and manager. Sisler's career batting average—an impressive .340 that equaled Lou Gehrig's—is among the all-time top 20 in major league baseball. It is said that for years Sisler faked not being able to hit a high inside pitch in order to trick opposing pitchers into throwing them when he was in trouble. His best years were 1920 and 1922, when he *twice* led the major leagues with .407 and .420 averages. When he was traded to the Washington Senators in 1927, Sisler's batting average fell below .250. He had some uncharacteristically inconsistent seasons before retiring

George Sisler

> *"If you pitched inside to him, he'd tear a hand off the third baseman, and if you pitched outside, he'd knock down the second baseman."*
>
> —*Chicago pitcher Ed Walsh on hard-hitting Nap Lajoie*

from playing in 1932, but even in old age, Sisler kept his eye on the ball by working as a scout for Branch Rickey. Sisler's son Dick played with the Cincinnati Reds for several years and managed the team from 1964–1965.

NAPOLEON LAJOIE

The graceful, good-looking French Canadian with the powerful bat not only was Cleveland's first sports hero, but also has been labeled the modern major league's first superstar. One of baseball's best players

in the first half of the 20th century, Lajoie was a Philadelphia Phillie when he led both leagues with a .422 batting average in 1901, and his .338 career average earned him one of the Baseball Hall of Fame's earliest berths. In 1905, he came to Cleveland as a player-manager and became so popular with fans that the team was renamed the "Naps" and the stadium had to be enlarged to handle the crowds. While at Cleveland, Lajoie finished a close second in a hotly contested batting average race with Ty Cobb and got his 3,000th career hit. The impressed Cleveland faithful declared Lajoie Day in 1912, and presented him an enormous horseshoe covered with more than 1,000 silver dollars. When Lajoie quit playing in 1916, he had collected 3,252 hits. He briefly managed teams in Toronto and Indianapolis, then retired from baseball, living comfortably on his wise business investments.

♦ JOE JACKSON

Joseph Jefferson "Shoeless Joe" Jackson was an unschooled left fielder from South Carolina who could neither read nor write. He did, however, know how to hit a baseball very, very well, and in the short span between 1911 and 1919, that ability would take him from the heights to the depths of professional baseball. Although Jackson's major league tenure from 1908–1920 seems almost antediluvian in relation to modern professional baseball, his career batting average of .356 is still the third highest in history, just trailing Ty Cobb (.367) and Rogers Hornsby (.358). From 1910–1915, Jackson played for the Cleveland Naps, the club where he reached his pinnacle with a .408 batting average in 1911. To the chagrin of the fans, the financially-pressed Cleveland club traded Jackson to the Chicago White Sox for some sorely needed cash. It was a fateful move that set the stage for Jackson's involvement in major league baseball's most infamous incident, the notorious "Black Sox" scandal. Jackson and seven other Chicago players

♦Joe Jackson was sensitive about his humble beginnings and illiteracy. During one game, when a heckling fan wanted to know if he could spell cat, Jackson hurled a contemptuous shot of tobacco juice toward him. Nonetheless, at the end of every baseball season, Jackson liked to migrate South to spend the winters back home. He always took every baseball bat he owned with him, allowing that northern cold was as harmful to bats as it was to ballplayers.

175

> "Benedict Arnolds! Betrayers of American boyhood. Not to mention American Girlhood and American Womanhood and American Hoodhood."
>
> —*Nelson Algren on the 1919 World Series between the Cincinnati Reds and the Chicago White Sox*

admitted to conspiring with gambler Arnold Rothstein and purposely losing the 1919 World Series to the Cincinnati Reds, presumably because of White Sox owner Charles Comiskey's niggardly pay checks. Although a jury found Jackson and the others not guilty of fraud, the scandal blackened not only the White Sox, but also all of major league baseball. Commissioner Kenesaw Mountain Landis banished Jackson and his cohorts from baseball for life, thus slamming the door on Jackson's almost certain entry into the Baseball Hall of Fame. Jackson was, however, immortalized in another, albeit far less flattering, way by the still-haunting phrase—"Say it ain't so, Joe"—shouted by the disillusioned little boy who waited outside his courtroom.

THE PERFECT PITCHERS:

J. LEE RICHMOND

Born in Ashtabula County in 1857, Richmond was a minister's son who had the benefit of an Ivy League education at Brown University. There he played on the baseball team and developed two curve balls that earned him a reputation as one of the nation's leading college pitchers. In 1879, Richmond signed with the Worcester, Massachusetts, team and became pro baseball's first regular left-handed pitcher, finishing his first season with 47 wins and a .368 batting average. Worcester joined the National League the next year, and on June 12, hosted the Cleveland club. Richmond was on the mound for Worcester, while player/manager Jim McCormick did the pitching honors for Cleveland. Richmond's left-handed delivery was then a novelty, and McCormick tried a then-novel strategy to compensate for it: loading the lineup with a string of right-handed batters. It didn't work. Cleveland only had one real prayer the whole day—a fifth inning base hit that was neatly neutralized by a Worcester right fielder's throw to first base—and Richmond fired off a string of strike-outs for a 1–0 final score. With Richmond's win, the National League had its first perfect game, only to claim another one just five days later when Providence's John "Monte" Ward bested Boston 5–0. Almost 25 years would pass before the National League would again find perfection in the formidable arm of Cy Young. Richmond got himself a medical degree while he played in the pros, but a bad arm ended his major league career by 1886. He went back to Ohio, gave up medicine for education, and took a position as a teacher at Toledo's high school. Richmond taught mathematics and science and, of course, he coached the baseball team.

CY YOUNG

Young pitched his second no-hitter on May 5, 1904, when his Boston Red Sox defeated the Philadelphia Athletics 3–0. But his mind was so focused on the mound that until someone handed him the last game ball, he was completely unaware that only 27 opposing batters had stepped up to home plate and that all 27 had stepped away. In not allowing any of them to reach first base, he had pitched the first perfect game of the twentieth century. Young later said he did it by mixing his pitches and getting some help from the fine fielding of his teammates. Here is how *Sporting Life* described the day: "Young's pitching was wonderful. He struck out eight basemen. Only six men went out on flies to the outfield, and only three on flies to the infield. There was not an error on the Boston side and Parent and Ferris had only seven grounders to look after. Young himself assisted on two grounders. There was not even a semblance of a hit."

ADRIAN "ADDIE" JOSS

Joss tossed his perfect game on October 2, 1908, in the midst of one of the hottest pennant races in major league history. The

> *"Cy Young lasted so long in the major leagues that it seemed they'd have to shoot him, on Judgment Day, with his baseball shoes still on."*
>
> —*Sportswriter Robert Smith*

Cleveland Indians were in a down-to-the wire contest for the American League title with the Detroit Tigers and Chicago White Sox. On September 24, the Indians were out in front by 2.5 games, and when they won again on the 26th, passions were so high that three bands led the fans in a half-hour victory march around the ballpark. When the Indians put Joss on the mound on October 2, he and the White Sox's Ed Walsh arm-wrestled through a game that *Sporting Life* called "the grandest pitcher's duel in history." By the eighth inning, Walsh had struck out 15 hitters and only given up four hits, one of which, an error, turned into a third-inning run for the Indians. Joss had help all day from the artful fielding of Nap Lajoie at second, and in the ninth inning, the White Sox put in three pinch-hitters in an attempt to save the game. Joss struck one man out, and the other two had hits that the Indians' fielders adroitly turned into outs. The final score was Indians 1, Chicago 0. Joss spent all of his nine major league seasons with the Indians, and ironically, he pitched a second no-hitter against the White Sox on April 20, 1910. He also won that game 1–0, making him the only major leaguer to pitch two nine-inning no-hitters against the same team.

♦ JIM BUNNING

A Xavier University graduate who grew up in the Cincinnati area, Bunning was pitching for Philadelphia on June 21, 1964, when his perfect game blanked the New York Mets 6–0. Bunning, along with his catcher Gus Triandos, had been traded by Detroit the year before, and it was moving to the National League that put his name in the record books *twice*. He was not only the first National Leaguer in 84 years to retire 27 consecutive batters, but also only the first pitcher in history to win a no-hitter in each of the major leagues: with the American League's Tigers, he had rendered the Red Sox hitless on July 20, 1958. Bunning's slider was the ticket to his 1958 no-hitter, and six years later, he brought the pitch into play again to ice his perfect game on a sultry New York night. The closest the Mets got to first base was in the fifth inning, when Jesse Gonder hit a line drive, but Phillies second baseman Tony Taylor made a diving catch and threw him out.

LEN BARKER

On May 15, 1981, Barker became the first Indian since Addie Joss to join the exalted ranks of the perfect game pitchers. Played in 40–degree temperatures on a rainy night, the game against the Blue Jays attracted only about 7,000 fans to Cleveland Stadium. But Barker worked magic on the mound with a sizzling curve ball, and 11 Blue Jays went out swinging in the last six innings. After Indians center fielder Rick Manning bagged a fly ball off of Ernie Whitt's bat for the last out, the Jays landed in the cellar 3–0. Barker's feat got him a champagne reception from his teammates, but little respect from his grandmother. When he called to tell her about his no-hitter, all she could say was, "Maybe next time you'll do a little better."

TOM BROWNING

Although Cincinnati is baseball's oldest ball club, no Reds pitcher had a perfect game until Tom Browning bested Los Angeles 1–0 on September 16, 1988. With excellent control and a variety of pitches, the left-hander only needed an hour and 51 minutes and 102 pitches (72 of which were strikes) to dismiss the 27 Dodgers. The game had the makings of a double no-hitter for both Browning and Dodgers right-hander Tim Belcher until the bottom of the sixth inning, when the Reds' Barry Larkin doubled and then scored on an infield single by Chris Sabo. Browning later surrendered the "lucky hat" he was wearing to the Baseball Hall of Fame, but he kept the ball that he threw to strike out LA's Tracy Woodson for the final out of that perfect night.

♦ *On June 21, 1964, Jim Bunning pitched the Phillies to a 6–0 no-hit win over the Mets. It was the first perfect game in the National League in 84 years, and only the eighth in baseball history. Bunning required 90 pitches, fanning 10. The date was Father's Day, and Bunning said he was angry that the Mets had given his family poor seats. "Next time I pitch here I hope I have better seats," he said.*

179

JERSEYS
A few retired uniform numbers worn by a few good men

NUMBERS RETIRED BY THE CLEVELAND BROWNS:

Quarterback Otto Graham, No. 14—the National Football League's Most Valuable Player in 1953 and 1955

Running back Jim Brown, No. 32—made All-Pro eight times, 1957–1961 and 1963–1965

Fullback Ernie Davis, No. 45—died of leukemia shortly after being drafted by the Browns in 1962

Defensive back Don Fleming, No. 46—electrocuted while working in an off-season job after the 1962 season

Offensive tackle/kicker Lou Groza, No. 76—made All-Pro six times and retired after the 1967 season

NUMBERS RETIRED BY THE CINCINNATI BENGALS:

Center Bob Johnson, No. 54—the team's first-ever college draft choice, 1968

NUMBERS RETIRED BY THE CINCINNATI REDS:

Manager Fred Hutchinson, No. 1—won the National League pennant in 1961; died of cancer, 1964

Catcher Johnny Bench, No. 5—the National League's Most Valuable Player in 1970 and 1972; World Series MVP, 1976

NUMBERS RETIRED BY THE CLEVELAND INDIANS:

Outfielder Earl Averill, No. 3—picked for the American League All-Star team six times in the 1930s; still leads the Indians in runs scored, triples, and home runs

Shortstop Lou Boudreau, No. 5—had seven All-Star game appearances in the 1940s; as player-manager, took the Indians to their last World Championship in 1948

Jim Brown

"Once, after a blast of six or seven yards, Brown was the first to regain his feet. When he got back to the huddle he was blowing hard—but the inert figures of three Giants marked the trail where he had passed, like the breadcrumbs on the forest path of Hansel and Gretel. For mercurial speed, airy nimbleness and explosive violence in one package of undistilled evil, there is no other like Mr. Brown."

—columnist Red Smith

> *"I don't think
> I was scared
> during the whole
> period. But I was
> a bit down most
> of the time.
> I had come from
> situations where
> I had always
> been accepted.
> I was alone a lot
> in major league
> baseball."*
>
> —*Larry Doby*

Pitcher Mel Harder, No. 18—played more seasons (20) for the Indians than any other player; picked for four All-Star teams in 1930s

Pitcher Bob Feller, No. 19—played in eight All-Star games (more than any other Indian) in the 1940s; still leads the team in shutouts, innings pitched, wins, and strikeouts

Outfielder Larry Doby, No. 14—became first black player in the American League when he joined the 1947 Indians; member of the 1948 Tribe that won the World Series.

NUMBERS RETIRED BY THE CLEVELAND CAVALIERS:

Forward Bingo Smith, No. 7—leads the Cavs in number of games and minutes played; second in field goals made; in 1979, was the last original Cavalier to leave the team

Guard Austin Carr, No. 34—leads the Cavs in points scored and field goals made; second in games and minutes played

Center Nate Thurmond, No. 42—considered one of pro basketball's greatest pivot men, he spent his last years in the National Basketball Association, 1975–1977, with the Cavaliers

MR. PIVOT

Akron native *NATE THURMOND*, the son of a rubber plant worker at Firestone, made all-city at Akron Central High School but he didn't get a lot of recruiting calls. At Bowling Green State University, he was selected for the Mid-American Conference first team in three consecutive years—1961–1963—and although the 6' 11" Thurmond made All-American center in 1963, his skills were still not widely recognized, probably because he concentrated on rebounding and defense. He set school records in rebounding—his three-year rebound total was 1,295—but his name barely appears among the scoring records. San Francisco, which already had a basketball giant by the name of Wilt Chamberlain, but with a good eye on Thurmond's defense, picked Thurmond in the first round of the 1963 NBA draft and never regretted it. In 11 years with the Warriors, Thurmond established himself as one of the all-time greats on defense. He was selected for the NBA's All-Defensive first team two times and made 1,000 rebounds during eight different seasons. Thurmond played the waning years of his impressive career—he is one of the few pros ever to pick up 10,000 points *and* rebounds—with the Bulls and Cavaliers. He is one of only six NBA players to have his jersey—the truly well-worn No. 42—retired by two teams: the Cavaliers and Golden State (formerly San Francisco).

> "I'm just the type of player that, when the game ends, people look at the boxscore and say, 'Oh, I didn't know he did that,' or 'Oh, did he score that many?' I'm not an exciting commodity."
>
> —Nate Thurmond

183

Ohio is not generally considered one of America's fast-lane states. Which only shows what the makers of such consider-ations really know. After all, Ohio is home to Jesse Owens, whose name has been synonymous with speed for over half a century. It's also home to Cincinnati fast-baller Rob Dibble (101 mph); the best roller coaster in the world, The Beast (64.77 mph); and Bobby Rahal, 1992's Indy Car Racing Champion (his average Indy lap: 170.722 mph). You need fast, we got fast.

SPEED MERCHANT

Jesse Owens finished first in 75 of the 79 races he ran at Cleveland East Tech High School, and his high school career ended in 1933 at the National Interscholastic Championships in Chicago where he set a world record of 20.7 seconds in the 220-yard dash and tied a record with 9.4 in the 100-yard race. In varsity competition he continually set and reset records. His time of 10.2 seconds in the 100 is *still* the OSU record. For all his accomplishments, college competition was just a primer for Berlin, where his four Olympic gold medals remain one of the Games' greatest accomplishments. His time of 20.7 seconds in the 200-yard dash was an Olympic record and his 10.3 100-yard dash tied the world record. Owens' records are more remarkable when considering the conditions under which he competed. Before starting blocks, synthetic tracks and light-weight racing shoes, the runners dug their own starting holes in the loose cinder tracks to plant their feet. The shoes were of cumbersome leather and were difficult to break in and easily waterlogged. And, instead of stopping the clock when the runner broke the tape, the judges waited until the runners' center of gravity—or sometimes even their back foot—crossed the finish line.

SOME LIKE IT HOT

Rob Dibble, Cincinnati Reds relief pitcher, is perhaps the premiere fire-balling pitcher in baseball. His pitches are continually in the 90 mph range, occasionally tipping 100 mph. Hitting a baseball has been called the most difficult act in sports, and Dibble's job is to make it impossible. A 100 mph pitch travels from the pitcher's hand to home plate in .41 seconds, or about 15 feet every tenth of a second. Facing Dibble, this is what the hapless batter must attempt to do: In the *first tenth of a second*, the batter must pick up the ball's likely flight path and judge what kind of pitch it is. In the *second tenth*, the batter must decide if the pitch is going to be a ball or a strike, and whether or not to swing. In the *third tenth*, get the bat ready and judge where in the strike zone the ball will be. In the *fourth tenth*, bat attempts to intersect the ball. Next stop, the dugout.

IN DRAG

In 1989, Dayton's Pat Dakin and his 1,950 pound, 5,000 horsepower, nitro-methane powered dragster was the top International Hot Rod Association point-getter. Top speed: 287 mph. This means he travels from 0–100 in less than a second and at the halfway point hits 240 mph. This is efficient enough to run the quarter-mile concrete strip in 5.01 seconds. A lot of this responsibility falls on Dakin's six-man team of mechanics that tunes the car between races. The secret is in adjusting the car's horsepower to the optimum level. Too much and he loses precious hundredths-of-a-second spinning the tires at the start. Not enough and he gets only a good view of his opponent's brake-chute. As a driver, Dakin has his own worries to contend with. Carefully anticipating the starting light—one false start and he is out—he opens the throttle, which releases the centrifugal clutch. Pulling four or five "G"s, he wrestles with the butterfly-shaped steering wheel to keep the car on its shortest distance between two points. A quarter of a mile and 15 gallons of fuel later, he shuts off the throttle and releases his parachute. Half a mile later, the car will come to a stop.

"Show us a placid closer and we'll show you a bus ticket to Class AAA."

—Paul Daugherty
on Ron Dibble

Electronic equipment on board monitors the car's performance. Then the automobile is taken back to the pits where the data is processed, adjustments made, and the car prepared for its next 1,320-foot trip.

BANDWRITING

The pomp and circumstances of The Ohio State University marching band's Script Ohio is not simply an elaborate game of follow-the-leader. Originally conceived and directed by band director Eugene Weigel in 1936, he adopted the French march, *Le Regiment*, and set about teaching his 120-piece marching band to spell. Both band and tradition continued to grow until the band membership reached its current number of 192, plus drum major. It was then necessary to pad the song in the middle, allowing the larger band more time to parade through the final "o." The latest version of the march takes three and a half minutes, though television viewers only see the final "i" and "o" formed during the last minute. The climax of the show is when a senior sousaphone player dots the "i." It's not known exactly how long it takes the selected member to get into position but it can't be long enough for the chosen marcher, and is remembered forever.

DOWNHILL RACER

How to best utilize a limited source of energy leads Heather Flury to spend an average of four hours each weekend from Thanksgiving to the end of June working on her car for the All American Soap Box Derby in Akron. In 1991, her work earned her third place in the Kit Car Junior Division—28.88 seconds down the 954-foot hill. Because the cars are powered only by gravity, contestants depend on subtle intricacies in design to gain precious hundredths of a second. One of the main derby rules is that the driver must construct his or her own car. For Flury's car, the steering mechanism is simply two cables connected to the front wheels. To stop the car there is a "scissor brake"—pushing a pedal drags a block of wood on the ground. When the car frame is compete, she adds iron weights to bring the car up to the maximum 206 pounds. Flury's four-foot-eleven frame contributes only 82 pounds and while the weights are necessary, she voices displeasure with them. "We painted the weights black and they collected all the heat from the sun," she said. "Now they burn my back when I sit in the car."

ROAD WARRIORS

If this isn't a record, you are still advised not to try it in your Citation: Tim Montgomery, a Fremont mechanic, and his partner "in civil disobedience," Ed Rahill, in 1984 drove a silver Trans Am coast-to-coast in 35 hours and 46 minutes—86 miles per hour. To the car, Montgomery added radials, quartz-halogen racing lights, an oil cooler, a 36-gallon racing fuel cell—and a month of grime so the Trans Am would look as inobtrusive as possible. Top speeds: 140 mph-plus on the Texas plains. Their only ticket: on I-71 outside of Cleveland. Trailed by a suspicious patrolman for miles, he finally cited them for non-use of turn signals.

THE ASPHALT JUNGLE

When Dublin's Bobby Rahal and the TruSports racing team won the 1986 Indianapolis 500, the car's average speed was 170.722 mph—including time spent for six or seven pit stops. The highest actual speed a TruSports driver has reached was when Pruit reached a tailwind-aided 230 mph on the Michigan 500 straightaway. As talented as the drivers are and as fast as the cars go, the race's outcome is generally determined in the pits. The TruSports pit crew can change four tires and pump 40 gallons of gasoline in 13.5 seconds.

> " *The next inkling I had that there might be problems was when I noticed the horizon was on the wrong side of the windshield.*"
>
> —*Art Arfons of Akron, after crashing at 610 mph on the Bonneville Salt Flats*

FASTEST OHIOAN

Everybody's favorite Man of Steel, Superman, of Metropolis and Cleveland, Ohio, is the fastest Ohioan, of course. How fast? As everyone knows, faster than a speeding bullet. And how fast is that? According to the NRA, the average speed for a U.S. service round—the M16—is 3,200 feet per second. Or 2,181.8 mph. Super could also leap tall buildings in a single bound but that's another story.

RISE AND FALL

In February of 1990, James "Buster" Douglas did the undo-able by knocking out then-heavyweight champion of the world and all-around tough guy Mike Tyson. In Vegas the oddsmakers were only taking bets on which round Buster would go down. A *Columbus Dispatch* sports writer, however, claimed Douglas could win the boxing upset of all time because he loved his mother, who died 23 days earlier. After the tenth-round knockout, Douglas was greeted in Columbus by 25,000 fans. It might not have been the fastest knockout but it was one of the fastest rides to prominence. A giant banner outside a Columbus health club proclaimed Buster sweated there. When it came time for Douglas to defend his title against Evander Holyfield, it was a media circus. Unfortunately, Buster's fall was as meteoric as his rise. In the third round, a Holyfield right sent Douglas away and all the banners and tee-shirts turned to canvas. His rise—and plummet—lasted just ten months.

MAJOR OHIO MOTION

PREHISTORIC—Mile-thick sheets of ice carved their way through what is today Lake Erie at a maximum speed of 330 feet a day.

1873—*Lip Pike* of the Cincinnati Reds beat a trotter in the 100-yard dash.

1891—Ohio's first car crash happened, in Ohio City, when *John Lambert's* self-built car hit a tree stump at 10 mph.

1903—*Barney Oldfield*, an Ohio farm boy, became first to achieve mile-a-minute speed in an automobile. The same year, the Wright Brothers trailed Oldfield's speed but defied gravity's pull and flew roughly 120 feet; during the 12-second flight, the plane reached 40 mph.

1904—*Harry Myers* received first Ohio traffic ticket, in Dayton. Speed: 12 mph.

1929—*Evar Swanson* of Cincinnati Reds ran bases in 13.3 seconds—slightly better than 18 mph. Time becomes standard for *Guinness Book of World Records*.

1979—Kings Island introduced *The Beast*, the longest wooden roller coaster in the world. Riders covered 7,400 feet of track in three minutes and 40 seconds. Cars reached maximum speed of 64.77 mph at the bottom of the ride's third hill.

MID-1980s—*Scott Miller* ran the 108 miles from Lexington, Kentucky, to Cincinnati in 16 hours. Later traveled from Cincinnati to North Carolina—378 miles—in six days.

1987—Dayton's *LaVonna Martin* was nation's fastest 100-meter woman hurdler with time of 12.8 seconds.

1988—At the Olympics, Ohio State University's *Butch Reynolds* broke 20-year-old world record in the 400 meters. Time: 43.29 seconds.

1992—*Lyn St. James*, Willoughby native, became the second woman to qualify for the Indianapolis 500 when she drove her Lola-Chevrolet around the two-and-a-half mile track at 220.150 mph and the 30th starting position.

1992—The *Other Paper* newspaper in Columbus conducted a reader's poll and learned readers would drive an average of 76.6 mph on the city's outerbelt if they knew they would not be ticketed. One reader's suggested speed: "Mach 1."

RAY CHAPMAN

The only major league player ever killed by a pitched baseball was Cleveland Indians shortstop Ray Chapman. On August 16, 1920, the Indians were in a race for the American League pennant when they went to New York to face the Yankees at the Polo Grounds. Yankee pitcher Carl Mays threw an underhand fastball that hit Chapman in the left temple. As was customary in those days, Chapman was not wearing a helmet, and he died a few hours later in a New York hospital. Chapman apparently had never seen the ball coming: the day was dark and drizzly, and the well-used baseball was dingy with dirt, spit, and tobacco juice. After Chapman's death, team owners banned spitballs and started the use of new, clean balls during games. His Cleveland teammates dedicated their remaining games to Chapman's memory, and in October, the Indians won their first World Series. Ironically, Chapman was seriously considering quitting baseball at the time of the accident. He had been married the year before to the daughter of a wealthy Cleveland businessman, and the couple was expecting their first child. The daughter born after his death only lived a few years, and his widow committed suicide.

ADRIAN "ADDIE" JOSS

The brilliant Cleveland pitcher—he had a perfect game against the White Sox's Ed Walsh in what many consider the ultimate pitchers' duel in 1908—was a Wisconsin native who began his career with the Toledo Mud Hens in 1900. From 1902–1910, he was with the Cleveland club, where he had four consecutive seasons in which he won 20 or more games. Joss completed an amazing 90% of the games he started, and among the all-time major league records, his career earned run average (1.88) is second only to his old rival Ed Walsh (1.82). During an exhibition game in 1911, Joss fainted. Doctors diagnosed pleurisy and sent him home to Toledo. Two days after Cleveland's season opener, he was dead of meningitis at age 31. Billy Sunday, the noted evangelist and baseball fan, conducted his funeral, reportedly the largest ever held in Toledo. Shortly afterward, the first all-star team was organized to play against the Cleveland club in a benefit for Joss's family. The American League brought out its best—including Walter Johnston, Tris Speaker, Ty Cobb, Jack Graney, Cy Young, Nap Lajoie, and Joe Jackson—and they raised $13,000 for the widow.

LOUIS SOCKALEXIS

One of the first American Indians to play major league baseball, Sockalexis was born on a Penobscot Indian Reservation in Maine in 1871. He played many sports very well, but excelled at baseball and had a better-than-.400 batting average at Holy Cross College. The potential greatness he showed in college, however, was undermined when he was expelled for drinking. Sockalexis turned professional in 1897, playing outfield for the Cleveland Spiders and hitting .338. His success was short-lived. Sockalexis sank into alcoholism, and by 1899, played in only seven games with the Spiders, who released him at the end of the season. No other team would have him, and Sockalexis took to begging and living on the streets. He died in 1913 at age 42, having let his considerable talent go to waste.

WILLARD HERSHBERGER

The Reds catcher who played second banana to Ernie Lombardi committed suicide midway though Cincinnati's pennant-winning 1940 season. On August 3, Hershberger had an exceptionally bad day at the ballpark in Boston. The Reds lost their game, and substituting for Lombardi, Hershberger had been hitless in five at-bats. Depressed over his performance, he went back to his hotel room and slit his throat. He was only 29 years old, and until that day, his career batting average had been an impressive—and promising—.316.

THURMAN MUNSON

Munson was born in Akron, raised in Canton, and adored in Yankee Stadium, where the barrel-chested catcher earned kudo after kudo in the 1970s. He was an All-American at Kent State and dropped out in 1968 to become the Yankees' number one draft choice. Two years later, Munson made history as the first catcher ever named the American League's Rookie of the Year. In 1971, he made only one error and that came on a play in which he was knocked unconscious. By 1976, Munson was not only the league's Most Valuable Player, but also the only man other than Lou Gehrig to be made the Yankee's team captain. He batted .529 in the 1976 World Series and tied the series record by getting six consecutive hits against the victorious Cincinnati Reds. Every season from 1975 through 1977, Munson batted beyond .300 and drove in at least 100 runs, and he was also a prime player in the Yankees' World Series championships in 1977 and 1979. In 1978, Munson built his dream house in Canton and moved his family back home to Ohio, where he could enjoy peace and privacy away from New York. He bought a jet airplane for commuting to Yankee Stadium, and while Munson was attempting to land at Akron-Canton airport on August 2, 1979, the plane crashed and Munson was killed.

SHANE CURRY

Shane Curry was a Cincinnati Princeton prep football phenom, sought by the largest football powerhouses in the country. At Miami University, he became a 6' 5", 270-pound defensive end for the Hurricanes, graduated in 1990 with a degree in marketing, and was drafted in the second round by Indianapolis. But in 1992, before the start of his second season where he was posited to become a mainstay of the rebuilding Colts, he was shot in the head while sitting in his truck in a parking lot outside a Cincinnati nightclub. His assailant was a 15-year-old, and the shooting seemed to have been caused by a brief argument over a parking space. Police said Curry did nothing to provoke it. "If you wanted to make a kid," his father said, "I don't know how you could make them any more perfect than Shane." His son's name, he said, came from the reluctant gunfighter in the classic Alan Ladd western.

STEVE OLIN AND TIM CREWS

Cleveland Indians' pitchers Olin and Crews had the tragic distinction of being the first two major league baseball players to be killed as the result of a single accident. On the night of March 22, 1993, during a break in spring training, they were fishing for bass on Little Lake Nellie near Winter Haven, Florida. Crews was driving the boat when it hit a dock at a speed of about 60 mph. Olin, who had led the Indians in saves the previous season, was killed instantly. Free agent relief pitcher Crews died the next day. Also on board was teammate Bob Ojeda, who was seriously injured, but recovered.

CLIFF YOUNG

Only a few months after the Olin-Crews accident, tragedy again visited the Cleveland Indians. Pitcher Cliff Young, a 29-year-old who had been with the club only a year, was killed on November 4, 1993, when the automobile he was driving hit a tree near his hometown of Willis, Texas. Having grown up poor, Young had pursued his dream of a major league career through nine long years in the minors. A former manager described him as "the kind of a guy who would go out and pitch a two-hit shutout and them apologize for giving up those two hits."

Chicago's Charlie Ross hits the first National League home run—off the Reds' "Cherokee" Fisher in Cincinnati, May 2, 1876

Red Grange plays in his last college football game— in Columbus against Ohio State, where the All-American and future Hall of Famer helped his Illini beat the Buckeyes, 14–9, in 1925

Satchel Paige makes his first appearance as a major leaguer— on July 9, 1948, when he pitched the Cleveland Indians to a 5–3 victory over Washington

Boston power-hitter Ted Williams becomes only the fourth player in baseball to get 500 home runs—June 17, 1960, in Cleveland Stadium

The Astros' Ken Johnson is the first pitcher to lose a complete-game no-hitter—defeated 1–0 by the Reds in Cincinnati, 1964

The Washington Senators' Ron Hansen hits the last triple play in the American League—executed July 30, 1968, in Cleveland Stadium against the Indians

San Francisco's Cesar Dario Guiterrez is the first major leaguer to get seven consecutive hits in seven times at bat during a single game—at Cleveland, against the Indians, June 21, 1970

Baseball's all-time best hitter Hank Aaron gets his first American League home run—April 18, 1975, in Cleveland Stadium, off the Indians' Gaylord Perry

Yogi Berra participates in his last baseball game— in Cincinnati, where the celebrated former Yankee catcher coached the Houston Astros against the Reds, October, 1989

Pitcher Nolan Ryan wins the last (and 324th) game of his 27-year career in the major leagues—August 15, 1993, when Ryan's Texas Rangers defeated the Indians, 4–1

Bruce Crampton is the first golfer to score a record-low 18-hole total of 63 in a Professional Golfers Association championship—at Akron's Firestone Country Club, 1975

Bobby Nichols' 271 is the lowest-ever 72-hole total in a PGA championship—at Columbus Country Club, 1964

Patty Sheehan's 64 is the lowest-ever 18-hole total in a Ladies Professional Golf Association championship—at Jack Nicklaus Sports Center, Kings Island, 1984

John Pezzin is the first professional bowler to achieve a record-setting 33 consecutive strikes—in Toledo, March 4, 1976

Billiards champion Willie Mosconi, who took the world title 14 times, pockets a world-record setting 526 consecutive balls—in Springfield, March, 1954.

"I never threw an illegal pitch. The trouble is, once in a while, I toss one that ain't ever been seen by this generation."

—Satchel Paige

HEISMAN TROPHY WINNERS
The eight Ohioans honored as the nation's best football players

Who gets it?

The college football player voted best in the country.

Who decides?

Former Heisman Trophy winners and reporters nationwide.

Who got the first one?

University of Chicago halfback Jay Berwanger in 1935, when the award was called the DAC Trophy and given by New York's Downtown Athletic Club to the best player east of the Mississippi.

When did the name and criteria change?

In 1936, after the death of Cleveland native John Heisman, a renowned college coach who was the club's athletic director.

The trophy:

It weighs 25 pounds and is worth about $2000.

1942, FRANK SINKWICH, GEORGIA TECH

Ohio's first Heisman winner was from Youngstown. Sinkwich was a flat-footed tailback with an uncanny ability to accelerate when he ran. His quick starts propelled him into becoming the top college rusher in 1941, and in 1942, he was the first collegiate football player to rush for more than 2,000 yards in one season. Sinkwich's running made him the runaway choice for the Heisman, but because of metal rationing during World War II, he received a certificate instead of a trophy. Playing for the Detroit Lions in 1944, Sinkwich's stellar rushing, passing, and punting season made him pro football's Most Valuable Player. In 1945, he was drafted by the Army and suffered a service football injury that prematurely ended his pro football prospects.

1944, LES HORVATH, OHIO STATE

Ohio State's coaching staff doubted that Horvath, a tailback from Parma, could even make the team in 1944: he weighed a mere 167 pounds and was also enrolled in a demanding dental program that meant he would have to be at Saturday morning labs before football games. But he rushed for a 5.6-yard average, scored 12 touchdowns, and took the Buckeyes to their first undefeated, untied season in almost three decades. Though hampered by injuries against Michigan, he scored two of the three touchdowns in the 18–14 win that gave the Buckeyes the Big Ten championship. Horvath played a few seasons with the Cleveland Browns and the Los Angeles Rams, for whom he later became the team dentist.

1950, VIC JANOWICZ, OHIO STATE

Only 5' 9" tall, and 189 pounds, Janowicz was a high school star and all-purpose player from Elyria who shined during his junior year in OSU coach Wes Fesler's single-wing offense. He played halfback as well as safety and even did the kicking for

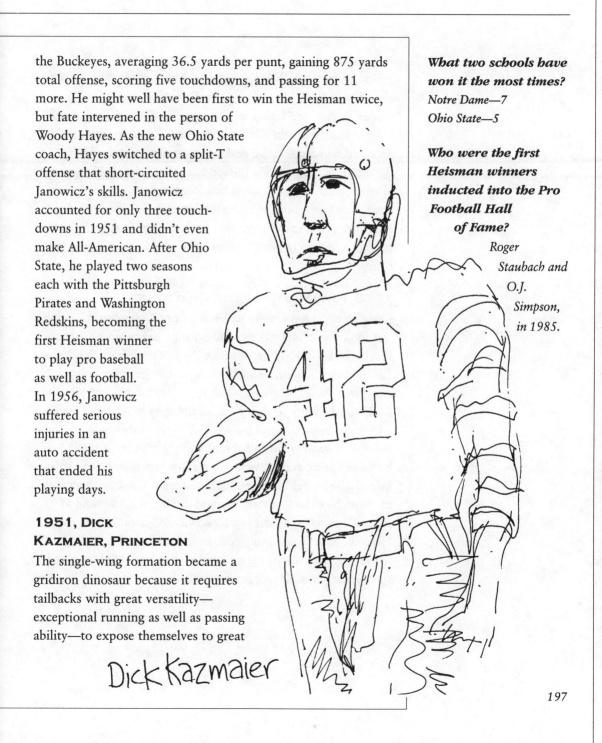

the Buckeyes, averaging 36.5 yards per punt, gaining 875 yards total offense, scoring five touchdowns, and passing for 11 more. He might well have been first to win the Heisman twice, but fate intervened in the person of Woody Hayes. As the new Ohio State coach, Hayes switched to a split-T offense that short-circuited Janowicz's skills. Janowicz accounted for only three touchdowns in 1951 and didn't even make All-American. After Ohio State, he played two seasons each with the Pittsburgh Pirates and Washington Redskins, becoming the first Heisman winner to play pro baseball as well as football. In 1956, Janowicz suffered serious injuries in an auto accident that ended his playing days.

1951, DICK KAZMAIER, PRINCETON

The single-wing formation became a gridiron dinosaur because it requires tailbacks with great versatility— exceptional running as well as passing ability—to expose themselves to great

Dick Kazmaier

What two schools have won it the most times?
Notre Dame—7
Ohio State—5

Who were the first Heisman winners inducted into the Pro Football Hall of Fame?
Roger Staubach and O.J. Simpson, in 1985.

197

vulnerability. Kazmaier proved himself one of the last of the multi-talented, single-wing tailbacks. Although the 5' 11", 170-pound man from Maumee was small, he was a first class runner, passer, and kicker who accumulated 4,354 yards total offense and 19 touchdowns at Princeton. Kazmaier took the Tigers to two consecutive undefeated, untied seasons, giving them rare ranking among the top ten college teams. His finest moment came in 1951, when he scored three touchdowns and passed for three more as Princeton lambasted Cornell 53–15. Kazmaier quit football after college, knowing his size and the fading formation in which he excelled would never yield a pro career.

1955, HOWARD CASSADY, OHIO STATE

Growing up in a down-on-its heels part of Columbus, Cassady was too poor to buy tickets to Ohio State games, so he used to sneak into Ohio Stadium to watch the Buckeyes play. At Central High School, he was a stand-out single-wing tailback, and coach Woody Hayes got him a scholarship to play with the Buckeyes. Cassady scored three touchdowns in his first game as a Buckeye freshman, and he—as well as the team—was off and running. Cassady made a habit of making big plays. In 1954, his interception and 88-yard touchdown run against Wisconsin helped give Hayes his first undefeated season and the Buckeyes the Rose Bowl and national championship. In his sterling 1955 season, Cassady scored 15 touchdowns and handily won the Heisman by a three-to-one edge over the runner-up. He signed with the Detroit Lions for a record-setting $15,000 bonus and spent eight years playing pro football.

1963, ROGER STAUBACH, NAVY

Born in Cincinnati in 1942, quarterback Staubach was a standout at Purcell High School and had more than 20 college scholarship offers. He picked the U.S. Naval Academy, where his skill as a runner and forward passer led the Middies to the 1964 Cotton Bowl and won him the Heisman Trophy in his junior year. After fulfilling his commitment to the Navy and serving during the Vietnam War, Staubach went to the Dallas Cowboys and was their starting quarterback from 1971–1979. Regarded as a class act on and off the field, Staubach was a bold and confident quarterback with a knack for transforming the Cowboys from underdogs to top dogs in the fourth quarter of a game. He executed 23 such victories, 14 of them during the last two minutes of overtime. Taking "America's team" to Super Bowl

"Nobody knows what Staubach is going to do but Staubach and God."

—Steve Gelman

Roger
Staubach

199

"He doesn't know anything about drugs. He thinks uppers are dentures."

—*Archie Griffin on Woody Hayes*

championships in 1972 and 1978, he was the National Football Conference passing leader five times. Staubach retired at the end of the 1979 season, having thrown for 22,700 yards and completed 153 touchdown passes in his pro career.

1974, 1975, ARCHIE GRIFFIN, OHIO STATE

Griffin has the distinction of being the only college football player to win Heisman Trophy twice, and he did it in consecutive years during Ohio State's gridiron glory days in the 1970s. Like Howard Cassady, Griffin grew up in Columbus, but his was a solidly middle class black family headed by devoted parents with an abiding faith in God and hard work. He made the first string, all-Ohio team his senior year at Eastmoor High and was heavily recruited by OSU coach Woody Hayes. Griffin was a small—5' 9" 185 pounds—but mighty running back who established a new Ohio State single game rushing record his freshman year and then broke that record as a sophomore. Setting a National Collegiate Athletic Association record by rushing at least 100 yards in 31 consecutive games, he was also the first college player to rush for more than 5,000 yards. After two decades, his 5,177-yard tally still ranks him fourth among college football's all-time leading rushers. Coach Hayes, along with most of Ohio, developed a genuine affection and regard for the level-headed, seemingly fearless Griffin, whose short legs carried the Buckeyes to a record-setting four consecutive Rose Bowls. Griffin's size finally did catch up with him when he went to the pros. He had eight respectable, but not stellar, seasons with the Cincinnati Bengals, then went back home to Columbus, where he works for the Ohio State athletic department.

1991, DESMOND HOWARD, MICHIGAN

Howard was the Wolverine's first Heisman winner in 51 years, following in the hoary footsteps of Tom Harmon by teaming up at Michigan with Elvis Grbac, his former teammate at St. Joseph High in Cleveland. Grbac the quarterback and Howard the wide receiver tied the NCAA record for scoring passes by a single duo, a winning combination that laid the foundation for the spectacular catches, runs, and punt returns that made Howard the second highest vote getter—2,077—in Heisman history during his junior year. It was a considerable irony, since in high school, Grbac mostly *handed* the ball to Howard—they completed exactly one pass. During his junior year at Michigan, however, Howard averaged 159 all-purpose yards per game and scored at least two touchdowns against nine of Michigan's opponents. When he first arrived at Michigan, the little—5' 9", 178 pound—tailback, the son of a Cleveland tool and die maker, went with the defensive backs, thinking he'd have a better chance there. But Bo Schembechler had seen him catch and when someone asked the coach how he was going to replace his top receiver, who was graduating, Schembechler said, "I've got this crafty little devil, Desmond Howard." Before he left Michigan, Howard's craft had broken nearly every major receiving and scoring record in UM's books, which dated all the way back to 1879. In the Ohio State game, Howard seized the moment twice: scoring a touchdown on a 93-yard punt return, then afterwards playfully mimicking the pose of the figure on the Heisman Trophy that he was only weeks away from winning.

NEVER ON SUNDAY

When the Cleveland baseball club played their first Sunday game on May 16, 1897, police arrested the players and the umpire at the end of the first inning. Owner Frank DeHaas Robinson bailed everybody out of jail, but an example was made of pitcher John Powell. He was found guilty of playing baseball on Sunday and had to pay a $25 fine.

STEALING HOME

Roy Rogers, Hollywood's' venerable "King of the Cowboys," claims he was born in a house once located on the spot now covered by second base at Riverfront Stadium in Cincinnati.

FROM THE DEAD

Woody Hayes was not Ohio State's first choice when the university went searching for a new football coach following Wes Fesler's firing in 1950. It wasn't until Missouri's Don Faurot decided to avoid the "Graveyard of Coaches" in Columbus that Hayes was considered for the job.

FASHION STATEMENT

On June 7, 1938, umpire Bill McGowan removed the Cleveland Indians' Johnny Allen from the pitching mound because the uniform sleeve covering his pitching arm was torn. Hotheaded Allen, who once beat an umpire for calling a balk, protested and had to pay a $250 fine. Indians owner Alva Bradley got Allen off the warpath by buying the ignoble garment and displaying it in a Cleveland department store, after which it was shipped off to the Baseball Hall of Fame.

FOWL

Don Schulze, a Cleveland Indians pitcher from 1984-1986, once tried to collect damages for injuries he claimed to have suffered after running into the San Diego Chicken. The matter was declared a fowl ball by a federal court, which ruled Schulze didn't have a leg—or perhaps, a drumstick—to stand on.

BALK

In 1953, 19-year-old Roger Maris, who as a New York Yankee would break Babe Ruth's single season home run record in 1961, passed up a football scholarship to accept a $15,000 signing bonus from the Cleveland Indians.

BUCKEYE BABY

Archie Griffin, the two-time Heisman Trophy winner who was arguably Ohio State's best running back and its most popular player ever, was born on the campus. He first saw the light of day in University Hospital, on August 21, 1954.

MAN OF STANDARDS

In 1873, Cornell President Andrew Dickson White struck an early—but futile—blow to college football when he would not allow the university's football team to play the University of Michigan in Cleveland. "I will not permit 30 men to travel 400 miles to agitate a bag of wind," he said.

GRIPPING DRAMA

The television age arrived in baseball on August 26, 1939, with a broadcast hosted by Red Barber from the Brooklyn Dodgers' Ebbetts Field. Cincinnati's hot pitcher Bucky Walters—he led the National League with 27 wins that year—stole the show when he demonstrated on camera how he held his curveball.

TRADITION

In 1932, the Cleveland Indians lost the first game they ever played in Cleveland Stadium, defeated by the Phillies 1-0. In 1993, the Indians lost the last game they ever played in the stadium, beaten by the White Sox 4–0.

1843—A *Mr. Watson* and a *Mr. White* open bathing houses on the Sandusky lakefront for well-to-do devotees of the new English fad of public bathing, that is, swimming. Ohio had many recreational swimmers before this date. However, they were unclad and thus unrecorded.

1878—*James West* opens several bathhouses near the beaches of Cedar Point. For many of West's day-tripping customers, the chances of getting their money's worth out of owning a bathing costume is so small that he rents them suits as well as rooms in which to change.

1880s—Bathing houses are the rage in big-city Cleveland. However, sound moral judgement requires that public bathing remain separate but equal between the sexes. Interracial bathing is beyond the pale.

1890s—The many bathhouses in Cleveland serve working immigrants who need not a soothing dip but a real bath after a day's hard work.

1910—Cedar Point builds what is purported to be "the world's largest bathhouse." Visitors can rent bathing suits, towels, and a changing room from a "key girl," who is paid 50 cents a day for her labors.

1913—Notre Dame footballers *Knute Rockne* and *Gus Dorais* find summer work at Cedar Point, and use their spare time on the beach to perfect the hitherto little-known "forward pass." Their new bomb routs Army in fall, Notre Dame jumps to national prominence, and footballers continue to practice at Cedar Point in summers.

1920—*Frances Cowells Schroth* is first Ohioan to earn place on U.S. Olympic Swim Team. She returns home with a silver and two bronze medals.

1926—Future movie star *Johnny "Tarzan" Weissmuller* dazzles the competition at a meet in the giant outdoor pool at Geauga Lake near Cleveland. In particular, he runs away with the 220-yard freestyle.

1928—At the Olympic Games, Ohioan *Walter Laufer* wins a silver medal in the back stroke.

1931—Urged on by former diver and new faculty member *Mike Peppe*, Ohio State establishes the men's swimming program, which will dominate the sport for the next 30 years. Under Peppe, Buckeye swimmers and divers take 33 major team titles, including 94 individual Big Ten championships.

1937—Impresario *Billy Rose* launches his much ballyhooed "Cleveland Aquacade." The aquatic fantasy, which features "aquadolls," "aquaclowns" and "aquadudes," plays a 7,000-seat lakefront amphitheatre. Backed by a locally recruited swimming chorus line, the stars of Cleveland's floating stage are *Johnny "Tarzan" Weissmuller* and Olympic rebel *Eleanor Holm*, a gold medal winner at the 1932 games who was banned from the 1936 team as too hot to handle. "I train on cigarettes and champagne," Holm said.

1939—Buckeye diver *Earl Clark* does the "twist" in mid-air, a manuever that becomes the basis of modern diving routines.

1943—OSU's grand-slam year: the Bucks win the Big Ten and both the indoor and outdoor AAU national titles.

1951—Buckeye swimmer and innovator *Dick Cleveland* takes up heavy weight training. Generations of swimmers yet unborn will grint through the Full Cleveland.

1952—Nine of 25 members of the U.S. mens' Olympic swimming and diving team are from OSU. So is the coach, the by-now legendary Mike Peppe. OSU's *Yoshi Oyakawa* and *Ford Konno* win gold medals.

1956—Buckeye divers win all top four places on the NCAA diving boards for the second time.

1957—*Al Wiggins* of Ohio State becomes the first swimmer to win national championships in three different strokes—the butterfly, backstroke, and freestyle. He is also an individual medley champion and a Big Ten medal of honor winner.

1960—*Sam Hall*, OSU's national three-meter diving champion in 1959, wins a silver medal in the Olympic games. In 1986, Hall is in hot water in Nicaragua where the self-proclaimed counter-terrorist is accused of spying by the Sandinista government. Hall is kicked out of Nicaragua in 1987.

1960—OSU diver *Juan Botella* demonstrates the "inward layout somersault," a dive said to be "mechanically impossible." The dive is still not listed in manuals. Botella wins a bronze in the 1960 Olympic Games as a member of the Mexican Olympic team.

1961—*Keo Nakama*, winner of four NCAA individual championships while at OSU between 1943-1945, becomes the first person to swim the treacherous Molokai Channel in Hawaii. Inside a towed shark cage, Nakama swims 26 miles across the notoriously choppy waters between the islands of Molokai and Oahu. In 1975, Nakama is inducted into the International Swimming Hall of Fame.

1969—The Cincinnati Pepsi Marlins swim club gains a new home, the "Keating Natatorium," funded by former Cincinnati swimmer *Charles Keating*, better known today as the man behind California's Lincoln Savings and Loan failure, which resulted created the largest pool of red ink in American banking history.

1976—Kenyon College swim coach *Jim Steen* establishes a women's swimming team, which finishes second place in the Ohio State small-college competition. The Kenyon Ladies go on to dominate state, conference, and national competitions.

1976—*Phil Boggs* from Akron wins the gold medal in springboard diving at the 1976 Montreal Olympics. Boggs, a three-time All-American, holds the 1973 world championship, was a 1971 NCAA three-meter champion, and introduces the reverse two-and-one-half somersault off the low board into NCAA competition.

1976—Seventeen-year-old *Tina Bischoff* of Columbus swims 22 miles across the English Channel in nine hours and three minutes, beating the 1964 mark of Britain's Barry Watson by 32 minutes.

1978—At age 65, *Walter Poenisch* of Columbus makes his 128-mile "Swim for Peace" from Cuba to Florida. Poenisch thus caps a career of endurance races and aquatic stunts such as towing a 30-ton boat carrying 63 passengers, a Dixieland Band, and assorted animals from the Columbus Zoo, over 250 feet up the Scioto River with his hands and feet tied.

1980—The Kenyon College Lords seize the national Division III crown, and defend their title for the 11th consecutive year.

1980—"Surf's Up," Ohio's first artificial surf park, opens in Sandusky, with 600 splashing swimmers paying good money to fight four-foot waves and white-water surf. Within ten years, there are some six fake oceans in the state, the greatest maritime resurgence since Ohio's last inland sea dried up 295 million years ago.

1983—The Cleveland Polar Bear Club, known for their annual winter dips in frozen lakes, goes into suspended animation. The Polar Bears brave the ice one last time to demonstrate their hardiness, as well as their lifesaving abilities (although who would be drowning in Lake Erie other than a Polar Bear is never made clear). In their swan swim, the last Polar Bears jump into Erie's 40-degree waters from the docks of Cleveland's Forest City Yacht Club. After the last goose-bump is swathed in terrycloth, the Polar Bears are extinct.

1984—The Lady Swimmers of Kenyon College began their reign as national champions in Division III swimming.

1984—OSU's Big Ten Champion diver *Kelly McCormick* wins the silver medal in three-meter diving in the summer Olympic Games in Los Angeles. McCormick goes on to win a gold medal in three-meter diving at the Pan-Am Games in 1987, and a bronze medal at the 1988 Olympic Games in Seoul.

1984—Former Cincinnati Pepsi Marlins swimmer *Mary T. Meagher* wins three gold medals at the Olympic Games in Seoul.

1985—*Jeff Sheard* of Columbus finishes the Manhattan Island Marathon Swim, a 29 1/2-mile route around the core of the Big Apple that is particularly grueling because of the trash floating in the water, and the currents.

1985—Ohio's largest municipal pool, the outdoor Lonnie Burton Pool on East 46th Street in Cleveland, opens. It is 150 feet wide and 300 feet long.

1986—*Betsy Mitchell* of Marietta sets a world record in the 200-meter backstroke: 2 minutes, 8.6 seconds. In the 1984 Los Angeles Olympics, Mitchell won the silver in the 100-meter backstroke and the gold in a 400-meter relay. Mitchell was a Cincinnati Pepsi Marlin before attending the University of Texas in Austin.

1987—Kenyon College Ladies' swimmer *Patty Abt* graduates from Kenyon with 23 NCAA swimming titles—more than any other person, in any division, in the country.

1989—Fifty-six-year-old *Yoshi Oyakawa*, a Southwest Ohio Masters competitor, former OSU swimmer, and Olympic gold medalist, sets a world record for his age group in the 50-meter and the 100-meter short course backstroke.

1990—Ohio State University's synchronized swim team wins the national championship for the 12th time. In the history of synchronized swimming, there have been 14 championships.

1990—Ohio ranks ninth among the states in residential in-ground swimming pools: 68,000.

1992—Cincinnati schoolboy *Joe Hudepohl* wins Olympic gold as member of 4x100–meter freestyle relay, and bronze in 4x200–meter freestyle relay.

1994—Ohio State's synchronized swim team wins national title again, its 16th; hasn't lost title since 1985.

1994—Kenyon swimmers again dominate Division III; men win 15th consecutive national title, women win 11th.

VANDER MEER, JOHNNY

Cincinnati Reds pitcher
(see page 22)
When Johnny Vander Meer went out to try for his
third no-hitter in a row, Cy Young came down from
his Ohio farm to see if the kid could break Young's
record of 24 straight hitless innings, which he set in
1904. Vander Meer came close; he went 21. And Young
went back to his
farm, still the
champ.

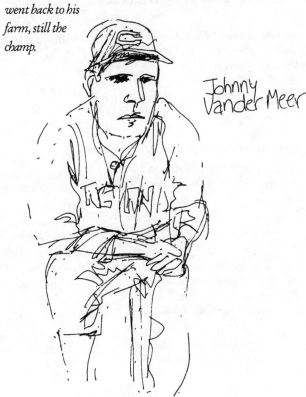

Johnny
Vander Meer

BIBLIOGRAPHY

Adler, Larry. *Football Coach Quotes.* Jefferson, NC: McFarland and Company, 1992.

Albers, Bucky. "Blond Beast lands at Kings Island" *Dayton Daily News*, February 1, 1990.

Alexander, Charles C. "Triple Play, Cleveland's Hall of Fame Triumvirate." *Timeline*, April-May, 1992.

Allen, Maury. *Baseball's 100, A personal ranking of the best players in baseball history.* New York: A&W Visual Library, 1981.

Anderson, Bob (Ed.). *Sportsource.* Mountain View, CA: World Publications, 1975.

Araton, Harvey. "There hasn't been a day we haven't missed him; Munson's family lived as he loved." *Akron Beacon Journal,* July 7, 1989.

Archdeacon, Tom. "Cassady Still A Hero." *Dayton Daily News*, October 12, 1991.

Asinof, Eliot. *Eight Men Out.* New York: Holt, Rinehart, and Winston, 1963.

Atkins, Harry. "Indians mourn fallen pitchers." *Dayton Daily News*, March 24, 1993.

Baker, William J. *Jesse Owens: An American Life.* New York: The Free Press, 1986.

Benningfield, Damond. "Ox, Mule and the Portsmouth Spartans Were the Pioneers of the Gridiron." *OHIO Magazine*, November, 1982.

Berlier, Nancy (Ed). *Cincinnati Days in History, A Bicentennial Almanac.* Cincinnati: The Cincinnati Post, 1988.

Boehm, David A. (Ed.). *The Guinness Sports Record Book*, 1987-88. New York: Sterling Publishing Co., Inc. 1987.

Bonenberger, Lynne M. "That Winning Season." *Ohio State Alumni Magazine*, September, 1992.

"Boston vs. Athletic at Boston May 5." *Sporting Life*, May 14, 1904.

Boudreau, Lou and Russell Schneider. *Covering All The Bases.* Champaign, IL: Sagamore Publishing, 1993.

Brady John T. *The Heisman: A Symbol of Excellence.* New York: Atheneum, 1984.

Brandt, John R. "Bottom of the Ninth." *Corporate Cleveland*, August, 1993.

Brondfield, Jerry. *Woody Hayes and the 100-yard War.* New York: Random House, 1974.

Brown, Paul with Jack Clary. *The Paul Brown Story.* New York: Atheneum, 1979.

Carruth, Gorton and Eugene Ehrlich. *Facts & Dates of American Sports.* New York: Harper & Row, 1988.

Carruth, Gorton. *What Happened When, A Chronology of Life & Events in America.* New York: Harper & Row, 1989.

Charlton, James (Ed.). The *Baseball Chronology, The Complete History of the Most Important Events in the Game of Baseball.* New York: Macmillan Publishing Company, 1991.

Clary, Jack. *Pro Football's Great Moments.* New York: Bonanza Books, 1983.

Cohane, Tim. *Great College Football Coaches of the Twenties and Thirties.* New Rochelle, New York: Arlington House, 1973.

Cohen, Richard with Jordan Deutsch and David Neft. The *Notre Dame Football Scrapbook*. Indianapolis: Bobbs-Merrill, 1977.

Collett, Ritter. "Devore's time with Dayton well done." *Dayton Daily News*, December 12, 1992.

"Country Patience Characterized Alston." *The Cincinnati Enquirer*, October 2, 1984.

Crossley, Linda S. "Oley's Idea Turns 50." *Ohio State Alumni Magazine*, March, 1988.

Curran, Bob. *Pro Football's Rag Days*. Englewood Cliffs: Prentice-Hall Inc., 1969.

Daly, Dan and Bob O'Donnell. *The Pro Football Chronicle*. New York: Collier Books, 1990.

Davis, George W. "Bulldogs, Tigers, a pigskin—and magic." *Akron Beacon Journal*, November 7, 1993.

Dickey, Glenn. *The World Series Since 1903*. New York: Stein and Day, 1984.

D'O'Brian, Joseph. "The Greatest Athlete in the World." *American Heritage*, July-August, 1992.

Dolgan, Bob. "Golden anniversary of a golden event." *The Plain Dealer*, July 14, 1991.

Eckhouse, Morris. "The Rivalry." *CLEVELAND Magazine*, October, 1987.

Edwards, Henry P. "With No Hit, No Base Game Joss Keeps Naps in Race." *Cleveland Plain Dealer*, October 2, 1908.

Eichenlaub, Jay. "Iron Man Eich." *OHIO Magazine*, August, 1985.

Eskenazi, Gerald. *Bill Veeck A Baseball Legend*. New York: McGraw-Hill Book Co., 1988.

"Ex-coach Woody Hayes dies." *Akron Beacon Journal*, March 12, 1987.

Flexner, Stuart Berg. *Listening to America, An Illustrated History of Words and Phrases from Our Lively and Splendid Past*. New York: Simon and Schuster, 1982.

Forbes, Dick. "Boxcar Bailey dies, but legend of Miami football star lives on." *Cincinnati Enquirer*, September 28, 1991.

Frank, Sid and Arden Davis Melick. *The Presidents: Tidbits and Trivia*. Maplewood, NJ: Hammond Incorporated, 1982.

Fulks, Danny. "Bevo's Odyssey." *Timeline*, February-March, 1992.

Fulks, Danny. "Hardwood Heroes." *Timeline*, February-March, 1988.

Grabowski, John J. *Sports in Cleveland, an Illustrated History*. Bloomington,IN: The Indiana University Press, 1992.

Green, Lee. *Sportswit*. New York: Harper & Row, 1984.

Laura, Haferd. "Super Ritual." *The (Akron) Beacon Journal*, January 21, 1989.

Harmon, Pat. "Even in L.A., Alston wasn't Hollywood." The *Cincinnati Post*, October 2, 1984.

Havighurst, Walter. *The Miami Years 1809-1969*. New York: G. P. Putnam's Sons., 1969.

Hayes, Woody. *You Win With People*. Columbus, OH: Typographic Print Co., 1973.

Homan, Marv and Paul Hornung. *Ohio State 100 Years of Football*. Columbus, Ohio: The Ohio State University, 1990.

Hoppel, Joe and Craig Carter. *The Sporting News Baseball Trivia 2*, St. Louis: The Sporting News Publishing Co., 1987.

Hoynes, Paul. "10 years ago, Barker was perfect." *Cleveland Plain Dealer*, May 15, 1991.

Hunter, Bob. "Hopalong bridged generation gap." *Columbus Dispatch*, November 12, 1989.

Husman, John Richard. "The First Perfect Game." *OHIO Magazine,* May, 1992.

Hyman, Mervin D. and Gordon S. White, Jr. *Big Ten Football: Its Life and Times, Great Coaches, Players, and Games*. New York: MacMillan Publishing Co., Inc., 1977.

James, Bill. *The Bill James Historical Baseball Abstract*. New York: Villard Books, 1986.

Justice, Richard. "These Days, the Bloom is Off Rose." *Washington Post*, March 26, 1989.

Katz, Marc. "Coach Woody Hayes dead at 74." *Dayton Daily News/The Journal Herald*, March 12, 1987.

Kimes, Beverly Rae. "The Dawn of Speed." *American Heritage*, November, 1987.

Knepper, George. *Ohio and Its People*. Kent, OH: The Kent State University Press, 1989.

Koehler, Michael D. *America's Greatest Coaches*. Champaign, IL: Leisure Press, 1990.

Kornacki, Steve. "Hard road to the Heisman." *Akron Beacon Journal*, December 14, 1991.

Lesko, Ron. "Irish eyes turn to BC Eagles." *Dayton Daily News*, November 16, 1993.

Limbacher, Jolene. "Football Players born, not made, in Massillon." *Akron Beacon Journal*, May 12, 1987.

Love, Steve. "It's M-M-Magnificent." *Akron Beacon Journal*, November 6, 1993.

Love, Steve. "Living Up to Greatness." *Akron Beacon Journal*, June 7, 1985.

Lovelace, Delos. *Rockne of Notre Dame*. New York: Putnam, 1931

Matthews, Peter. *The Guinness Book of Records, 1994*. New York: Facts on File, 1993.

McDonald, Joe. "Pete Rose out of prison; community service next." *Dayton Daily News*, January 1, 1991.

McDonough, Will. "The game's greatest innovator." The *Boston Sunday Globe*, August 11, 1991.

McKay, Bob. "Big Klu." *OHIO Magazine*, May, 1983.

McKay, Bob. "Master." *OHIO Magazine*, May, 1988.

Media Guides of college, university, and professional teams in Ohio

Mellen, Joan. *Bob Knight, His Own Man*. New York: Donald I. Fine, Inc., 1988.

Mercurio, John A. *"Record Profiles of Baseball's Hall Of Famers, All The Records Set by Baseball's Greatest Players."* New York: Harper & Row Publishing Co., 1990.

Meserole, Mike (Ed). *The 1994 Information Please Sports Almanac*. Boston: Houghton Mifflin Company, 1994.

Miller, Rusty. "Janowicz shoulders heavy load." *Dayton Daily News*, August 23, 1991.

Montgomery, Jim. "Oiler's offense first devised here." *The Cincinnati Enquirer*, January 6, 1991.

Nash, Bruce and Allan Zullo. *The Baseball Hall of Shame 3*. New York: Pocket Books, 1987.

Nash, Bruce and Allan Zullo. *The Baseball Hall of Shame's Warped Record Book*. New York: The MacMillan Publishing Company, 1991.

Natali, Alan. "Tigertown." *OHIO Magazine*, September, 1983.

Natali, Alan. "Woody." *OHIO Magazine*, May, 1987.

National Collegiate Athletic Association. *NCAA Football's Finest, All-Time Great Collegiate Players and Coaches*. Chicago: Triumph Books, 1991.

National Football League. *The Super Bowl, Celebrating a Quarter-Century of America's Greatest Game*. New York: Simon and Schuster, 1990.

Nemec, David. *The Great American Baseball Team Book*. New York: Plume, 1992.

Newhouse, Dave. *Heisman*. St. Louis: The Sporting News Publishing Co., 1985.

"Nicklaus blows away Seniors at PGA." *Dayton Daily News*, April 13, 1990.

Nicklaus, Jack, with Ken Bowden. *On and Off the Fairway*. New York: Simon and Schuster, 1987.

Official 1992 NCAA, National Collegiate Athletic Association.

Okrent, Daniel and Harris Lewine (Eds). *The Ultimate Baseball Book*. Boston: Houghton Mifflin Company, 1988.

Osinski, Bill. "Canton—the midwife of the NFL." *Akron Beacon Journal*, July 22, 1984.

Paolercio, Michael. "Browning Pitches Perfect Game." *The Cincinnati Enquirer*, September 17, 1988.

Park, Jack. *Ohio State Football, The Great Tradition*. Columbus, OH: The Lexington Press, 1992.

Pearson, Richard. "Waite Hoyt, Yankee Pitcher, Cincinnati Announcer, Dies." *The Washington Post*. August 26, 1984.

Peterson, James. Th*e Four Horsemen of Notre Dame*. Chicago: Hinckley and Schmitt, 1959.

Peterson, Robert. *Only the Ball Was White*. Englewood Cliffs, NJ: Prentice Hall, 1970.

Polner, Murray. *Branch Rickey, A Biography*. New York: Athenum, 1982.

Porter, David L. (Ed). .*"Biographical Dictionary of American Sports Baseball."* New York: Greenwood Press, 1987.

Porter, David L. (Ed). *"Biographical Dictionary of American Sports Basketball and Other Indoor Sports."* New York: Greenwood Press, 1989.

Postman, Andrew and Larry Stone. *The Ultimate Book of Sports Lists*. New York: Bantam, 1990.

Rappoport, Ken. *Wake Up The Echos-Notre Dame Football*. Huntsville, AL: The Strode Publishers, 1984.

Rathet, Mike and Don R. Smith. *"The Pro Football Hall of Fame Presents Their Deeds and Dogged Faith."* New York: Rutledge Books Balsam Press Inc., 1984.

Reichler, Joseph L. (Ed.). *The Baseball Encyclopedia.* New York: MacMillan Publishing Company, 1985.

Reichler, Joseph. *Baseball's Great Moments.* New York: Crown Publishers, Inc., 1974.

Reidenbaugh, Lowell. *Cooperstown Where Baseball Legends Live Forever.* St. Louis: The Sporting News Publishing Company, 1983.

Reidenbaugh, Lowell. *The Sporting News Selects Baseball's 50 Greatest Games.* St. Louis: The Sporting News Publishing Co., 1986.

Rickey, Branch with Robert Riger. *The American Diamond, A Documentary History of the Game of Baseball.* New York: Simon and Schuster, 1965.

Ritter, Lawrence and Donald Honig. *The Image of Their Greatness, An Illustrated History of Baseball from 1900 to the Present.* New York: Crown Publishers, Inc. 1984.

Rockne, Knute. *The Autobiography of Knute Rockne.* Indianapolis: Bobbs-Merrill Company, 1930.

Rosaforte, Tim. "2 who still have the drive." *Dayton Daily News,* January 22, 1990.

Rose, Pete and Roger Kahn. *Pete Rose: My Story.* New York: Macmillan Publishing Co., 1989.

Roseboom, Eugene H. and Francis P. Weisenburger. *A History of Ohio.* Columbus, OH: The Ohio Historical Society, 1988.

Schembechler, Bo and Mitch Albom. *Bo.* New York: Warner Books, Inc., 1989.

Schoor, Gene. *100 Years of Notre Dame Football.* New York: William Morrow and Company, 1987.

Simms, Greg. "Playing in his father's Shadow." *Dayton Daily News,* January 31, 1992.

"Simply Perfect." *Sports Illustrated,* September 26, 1988.

Smith, Don R. *Pro Football Hall of Fame All-Time Greats.* New York: Gallery Books, 1988

Smith, Robert. *Baseball in America.* New York: Holt, Rinehart, and Winston, 1961.

Snow, Richard F. "Barney Oldfield." *American Heritage,* February, 1977.

Snypp, Wilbur and Bob Hunter. *The Buckeyes, A Story of Ohio State Football.* Tomball, TX: The Strode Publishers, 1988.

Sowell, Mike. *The Pitch That Killed.* New York: Macmillan, 1989.

Sperber, Murray. *Shake Down The Thunder-The Creation of Notre Dame Football.* New York: Henry Holt and Company, 1993.

Spink, J.G. Taylor. *Judge Landis and Twenty-five Years of Baseball.* New York: Thomas Y. Crowell Co., 1947.

"Sports Editor Si Burick dies at age 77." *Dayton Daily News,* December 11, 1986.

Sports Illustrated 1994 Sports Almanac. New York: Little, Brown and Company, 1994.

Staubach, Roger with Sam Blair and Bob St. John. *Staubach, First Down, Lifetime to Go.* Waco, TX: Word Incorporated, 1974.

Stuhldreher, Harry. *Knute Rockne-Man Builder.* Philadelphia: Macrae Smith Company, 1931.

Sullivan, George and Barbara Lagowski. *The Sports Crumudgeon.* New Yor: Warner Books, 1993.

The Lincoln Library of Sports Champions. 20 Volumes. Columbus, OH: Frontier Press Company, 1981.

The Ohio Sports Almanac. Wilmington, OH: Orange Frazer Press, 1992.

Trebilcock, Bob. "A Flag Down on the Play." *OHIO Magazine,* December, 1985.

Van Tassel, David D. and John J. Grabowski (Eds.). The *Encyclopedia of Cleveland History.* Bloomington: Indiana University Press, 1987.

Vare, Robert. *Buckeye, A Study of Coach Woody Hayes and the Ohio State Football Machine.* New York: Harper's Magazine Press, 1974.

Voigt, David Quentin. *American Baseball.* Norman, OK: University of Oklahoma Press, 1966.

Wallace, Francis. *Notre Dame: Its People and Legends.* New York: David McKay Company, 1969.

Weywand, Alexander M. *Football Immortals.* New York: The MacMillan Company, 1962.

Wheeler, Lonnie and John Baskin. *The Cincinnati Game.* Wilmington, OH: Orange Frazer Press, 1988.

White, Gordon S. "Bunning Pitches a Perfect Game; Mets Are Perfect Victims, 6 to 0." *The New York Times,* June 22, 1964.

Wurman, Richard Saul. *Baseball Access.* Los Angeles: Access Press Ltd., 1984.

Young, Mark (Ed.). *The Guinness Book of Sports Records, 1993.* New York: Facts on File, 1993.

Zimmerman, Paul. "Sportman of the Year Don Shula." *Sports Illustrated,* December 20, 1993.

LOMBARDI, ERNIE

Cincinnati Reds Hall of Fame catcher

(see pages 35, 91)

He caught Johnny Vander Meer in his back-to-back no-hitters.
Years later, asked what he recalled about them,
Lombardi said, "Nothing. He didn't even
buy me a Coke."

Ernie
Lombardi

INDEX

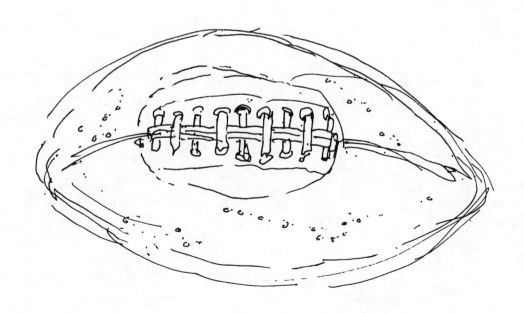